Tiny
Victory
Gardens

Tiny
Victory
Gardens

*Growing food
without a yard*

Acadia Tucker with Emily Castle

STONE PIER
PRESS

Stone Pier Press
San Francisco, California

ISBN: 9781734901108
Library of Congress Control Number: 2021953046

Names: Tucker, Acadia, author. Castle, Emily, illustrator. Ellis, Clare, editor.
Title: Tiny Victory Gardens: Growing food without a yard

Printed in the United States of America

First printing: March 2021
23 22 21 20 19 5 4 3 2 1

Cover design/illustration by Alex Robbins

Designed and set in type by Abrah Griggs

Contents

THE MIGHT OF TINY GARDENS

Driving across the country with a sprig of basil riding shotgun heralded the start of my love affair with container gardening. My long trip home to New England, after spending six years farming in Washington State, wasn't the first time I'd grown food in pots. But the way it came about shifted how I thought about container gardening.

The day before I left, I'd spent most of my time cleaning up the greenhouses and saying goodbye to the two friends I'd teamed up with to turn a neglected, overgrown patch of dirt into a market farm that produced more than two hundred different fruits, vegetables, and herbs. On my last walk past the asparagus we'd worked so hard to grow and the lettuce our clients couldn't get enough of, I swiped some

Plastic pot with basil: Plastic pots are cheap and readily available, which makes them a popular container choice—and why I used one to rehome my basil on the fly.

basil, just because. As I was closing the farm gates for the last time, it occurred to me that I could take that basil with me. I picked up the first plastic pot I saw, transplanted the basil, and we hit the road.

I'm not going to tell you that little plant survived the trip across snow-covered mountains, flat, barren deserts, endless wide plains, and the long final stretch to the East Coast. But while it was with me, right up until I'd driven about halfway across Oklahoma, I still had a little bit of the farm with me, which was comforting.

The I-can-take-it-with-me benefit of growing food in planters has always appealed to me. I'm a longtime renter and that basil plant isn't the only one I've packed up on my way to a new home. But the harsh New England winters, first in New Hampshire and then in Maine, where I eventually settled and now work as a grower, helped me appreciate container gardening anew.

At the end of my first growing season back East, after I'd turned the turf behind my Dad's house into a garden, I started bringing home the vegetables I couldn't bear leaving behind, like late-season cherry tomatoes and the potted up lettuce I didn't want to lose to frost. My collection of rehomed vegetables lived on the kitchen table for about a week—charming, but very impractical. In thinking about where to keep them long-term, or at least for as long as they'd continue to bear fruit, I found myself reimagining my indoor space as a climate-controlled mini-farm.

Among the first changes I made was to bring in a deep, wide container. I pushed it against a sliding glass door to take advantage of the southern light, filled it with an organic potting mix, and transplanted the tomatoes and lettuce. A week later, I brought in another big container and planted beets.

Over the course of that first winter, I lined my window sills with potted herbs including thyme, oregano, and rosemary, eventually slipping the generic plastic pots into patterned ceramic ones that accented my pale blue kitchen walls. I hung baskets on used curtain rods for the cascading mini cucumbers I like to pickle. And I realized a long-held dream of growing my own tropical fruit by potting a banana and a lime tree and tucking both into the dining room—the warmest room in the house.

But the moment I fully embraced container gardening was sometime in the spring, when I caught a glimpse of how much mightier it could be than I'd presumed. A friend dropped by with some cilantro and, since I was short on pots, I stuck it in with my beets. It was my first experience pairing up plants in a container, albeit on a micro scale, and it proved to be a turning point. I continued to experiment with various pairings, and once I saw how much food I could get out of a single pot, I was all in.

I've wanted to grow food for as long as I can remember, so the chance to farm in the Pacific Northwest was kind of a dream come true. It helped to be a little starry-eyed. Early on, we ran into all the usual challenges experienced by growers with big ambitions, very few resources, and a revenue model reliant on growing as many vegetables as possible in one short growing season. Our precarious situation was made more so when almost half of our first crop turned out to be too stunted and chewed up by pests to sell.

But the setback changed the way I grow food, and within two years, we were harvesting thousands of pounds of food from just two acres— more than enough to feed our small community. Our plants developed sufficient resilience to help us better weather the droughts and near-violent rainstorms that are now part of the Pacific Northwest's warming landscape. We were able to save money on watering, and on synthetic fertilizers and pesticides since we'd stopped using them.

The secret to our success was cultivating healthy soil by adopting regenerative growing practices, which mimic nature and allow organic matter to build up in the soil. We gave up tilling, planted cover crops to protect against soil erosion, and treated our land to big helpings of compost. In doing so, we fed the community of living creatures that thrive off organic matter, from microscopic bacteria to soil giants like worms and millipedes.

A happy byproduct of microbe-rich soil is its ability to capture and store carbon. This is the reason grasslands hold about 20 percent of global carbon stocks, and forests capture about one-quarter of global carbon emissions every year. (Though deforestation is undermining this effect.) It's also how we turned our farm into a carbon sink.

The promise of building out a foodscape large enough to help cool our planet inspired my first two books, which focus on backyard gardening using regenerative practices. I've since learned that container gardening has environmental benefits as well.

Admittedly, small potted gardens will never become carbon-sucking powerhouses. Even raised beds are a stretch. Soil expert Eric Toensmeier was able to offset the annual carbon emissions of one adult on only a tenth of an acre packed with deep-rooted perennial plants. Impressive, but that translates to something like 136 four-by-eight-foot raised beds.

Still, filling your planter with compost-rich potting mix, alive with beneficial soil organisms, means your plants will likely be easier to tend to and more nutritious. At the very least, you can spend less time watering and ditch the fertilizers and insecticides that do far more harm than good.

Growing food in containers is also an excellent way to support pollinators, which have taken a big hit in recent years thanks in part to our warming planet and overuse of pesticides. Planting flowers and food in pots creates a safe zone for pollinators in urban environments where food is already scarce, as well as in suburban areas rolling in manicured lawns, which are biological wastelands.

Many pollinators are small and can't fly very far. As their habitats shrink, they become isolated from food and each other. Planting a cross-country corridor of balcony crops, rooftop oases, and backyard container gardens can help these beneficial insects find enough food to survive so that they, in turn, can pollinate our food.

The fact that container gardening allows just about anyone to grow a decent amount of food, no backyard required, leads to another benefit: While growing food in pots may not do much to mitigate climate change, it can help us adapt to it.

In two recent reports, scientists on the UN's Intergovernmental Panel on Climate Change (IPCC) found that climate change, combined with the "unprecedented rate" of exploitation of the world's land and water resources, is putting an immense strain on crop production. The researchers ticked off the various ways fast-rising temperatures are threatening the productivity of farmland, among them, record-setting hurricanes and flooding in the Southeast, blistering heat waves and torrential rains in the Midwest, and extended periods of drought and intense heat in California, which is being incinerated by multiplying and ever-widening wildfires.

This is scary stuff, and just about everyone knows we have to act faster to head off the worst of it. In the meantime, it's not a bad idea to prepare for an increasingly uncertain world by learning how to grow food. Cultivating your own food source is a meaningful way to promote resilience in your household and, by sharing your knowledge with neighbors—along with the fruits and vegetables of your labors—it can do the same for your community. This is already happening in areas that often struggle economically, like Detroit and the Bronx, where community gardening, which provides an affordable source of fresh food for many locals, is thriving.

My own small farm in Point Roberts, Washington, became an example of food resilience when the pandemic closed the Canadian border, blocking off the town's primary source of food and support. Fortunately, the residents had taken ownership of The Coop, as we called it, and kept it going. The raised beds, mended greenhouses, and planted fields we'd left behind produced enough fresh food to generously supplement what the town's single grocery store could supply.

The ultimate in food security—and I may be getting ahead of myself here—may be the ability to grow at least some of our food indoors. Big swaths of the country already experience smoky air and extreme heat on a regular basis.

Learning how to grow your own food can promote resilience within your own family and community.

Setting up a climate-controlled indoor farm that buffers against weather swings isn't all that crazy. I'm already doing it to an extent myself. Adding to the appeal is that all those plants can make stuffy interiors a little fresher, thanks to the upcycling of oxygen and carbon dioxide that's part of the ordinary process of photosynthesis.

In chaotic times, it's easy to become nostalgic for the last time US citizens came together in force to grow food. During World Wars I and II, the government pitched victory gardening as a way for Americans to do their patriotic duty, and leaned on slogans like "Food is Fighting," and "Be a Soldier of the Soil." Eager to do something, *anything*, to help the cause, people rallied. They planted vegetables in yards, abandoned city lots, and schoolyards; in pots on stoops, rooftops, and fire escapes. By 1943, the nearly 20 million victory gardens across the country were growing 40 percent, or 80 billion pounds, of the nation's food.

In this book, you'll find the tools and instructions needed to grow your own tiny victory garden. One that can supply you with as much, or as little, food as you'd like, grown in a way that helps the planet. All you really need to grow food in containers is a patch of sun. This book will teach you how to make the most of that light, and build more resilience into your life.

I take heart from visionaries like Paul Hawken, co-founder of Project Drawdown, a nonprofit that tracks climate solutions. He sees enormous potential in the food sector's ability to mitigate climate change. The keys will include reducing food waste, adopting plant-rich diets, and changing how we grow food, and as Hawken says, "farmers, urban growers, backyard gardeners, and all of us eaters can, and will, lead the way."

LIVING SOIL

The first time I walked around the two-acre property that I'd signed on to farm sight unseen, I was a little anxious. Looming at one end of the field were three tattered greenhouses filled with random debris, their ripped plastic siding flapping loudly in the wind. The land, which once grew potatoes and apples, had become overwhelmed by monster stocks of prickly thistle and chicory. The wooden fence circling the site needed serious mending to keep away neighboring horses. And the soil? I could barely find it.

I bent down to pull up a clod of turf to see what we were dealing with. Pea-sized pebbles rained from the entangled roots. The stuff was so hard and compact I could not make a dent in it, even after jumping up and down on my shovel. Hidden under a thin layer of grass was

Hollow tree stump: This stump was all that remained of a tree that once graced a house I rented. By the time I arrived, it had become pretty spongy. I hollowed it out further, added some potting mix, and it very quickly turned into a wonderful bed for chives, one likely teeming with microbes.

construction fill, which had been trucked in years earlier to level about half the property. I wanted to scream.

But giving in to despair was not an option. It was the middle of winter and we had to plant food first thing in the spring. We didn't have the time or money to remove the fill. So we decided to skirt the dirt problem entirely, and build raised beds out of cedar planks.

For the next two months we hauled in a series of heavy, rough-edged cedar timbers, cut them to size, and screwed them into place. The work was every bit as hard as it sounds. It ate up most of every day, and left us spent by the time we broke for dinner. But by March, we'd managed to build thirty four-by-eight-foot beds. Now all we had to do was fill them.

At first it was as easy as we'd expected. We found an affordable supplier of dirt, hired a dump truck to drop off twenty-eight yards of it, and reached out to the community to see if they could help. Armed with wheelbarrows, shovels, and a generous supply of goodwill, neighbors and friends showed up to help fill those cedar beds. Thanks to all their support, it only took one very long day to get the job done.

We celebrated by turning on the ancient overhead sprinkler system in the greenhouse and dancing under the spray. Over the next few days, my partners and I quickly planted baby lettuce, spinach, and arugula. It was the start of our first crop of spring greens. Then we turned to our weed-choked fields.

We cleared out the chicory, thistle, and dandelions as best we could, relying on brush hogs and hand shears to do the job. Then we built our own fresh soil on top of what remained. We did it by sheet mulching, which involves building a great big heap of fresh yard waste, alternating brown materials, including shredded leaves and old hay or straw, with green, like untreated grass clippings and kitchen scraps collected from around town. Afterward, we spread a little compost on top of the pile and planted long rows of squash, corn, and cabbage seedlings.

We didn't have to wait long to see the stark difference between the store-bought soil and the living soil we'd made ourselves. The squash,

THE BENEFITS OF LIVING SOIL

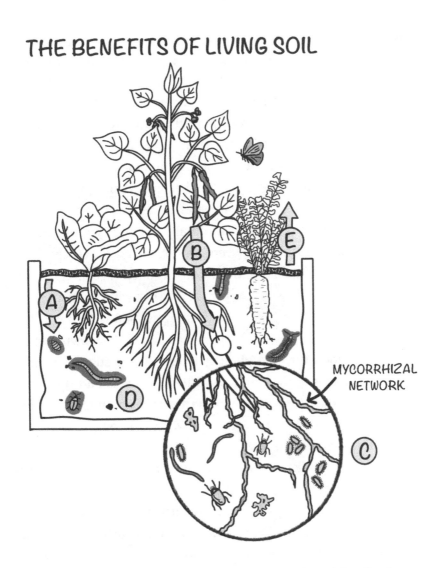

MYCORRHIZAL NETWORK

A. Organic material, like compost, applied to soil forms the base of the soil carbon cycle, feeding all organisms, large and small.

B. Through photosynthesis, plants convert carbon dioxide into carbon-rich sugars that flow down through their roots and attract and feed soil organisms.

C. The rhizosphere, or area around a plant's roots, is filled with small soil organisms attracted by the buffet of carbon-rich sugars. They break down organic matter, and in the process, release nutrients for plants to use. A vast network of mycorrhizal fungi also helps plant roots access nutrients and water, and communicate with each other.

D. Soil giants like earthworms and beetles move through the soil, creating channels that aerate it and promote good drainage, and also eat organic matter.

E. Some carbon from the soil is lost due to soil respiration and decomposition.

corn, and cabbage grew in nicely—sturdy, tasty, and destined to make our customers happy. But over in the cedar beds, those poor salad greens were stunted, peppered with pinholes, and so bitter it was clear they hadn't gotten enough water. The dirt we'd ordered was "affordable" for a reason; it apparently contained none of the organic matter, or compost, that plants need to flourish.

There's so much going on below ground that a gram of healthy soil can contain more than one billion bacteria, many yards of fungi strands, thousands of protozoa, and even more. To date, only a small fraction of this underground community has been identified, and even fewer of its residents have been studied. What we do know is that we need microbial organisms to build soil fertility, curb disease, fight pests, and lock in moisture. Frankly, we'd be lost without them.

One way these tiny organisms help grow food is through their symbiotic relationship with plants, which create their own carbon-based sugary food through photosynthesis. These sugars are what feed plants as they grow, and a significant number end up underground, where they attract and nourish mycorrhizae, nitrogen-fixing bacteria and protozoa, along with earthworms, pillbugs, nematodes, and other soil organisms.

This may seem like a waste of energy for plants but in exchange they get access to nutrients and protections that only these microbes can deliver. When they die, these organisms leave behind carbon, which remains in the soil for as long as it's undisturbed. This is how plants help soil capture and store carbon.

In almost every talk I've ever given on growing food, I've spent most of my time preaching the benefits of compost. I've seen it turn around struggling gardens, revitalize beaten-down, mono-cropped and chemically fertilized farms, and enable people with absolutely no growing experience to become small-scale farmers. Without well-fertilized soil chock-full of microbial activity, no amount of weeding, seeding, watering, or sunlight will save your plants.

Once we started lavishing compost on those long-neglected fields, everything changed. The dead leaves, roots, and food scraps we piled up invited billions of soil critters, which ate their way through it, breaking it all down into small pieces. They took the nutrients they needed, and left behind the rest to feed our plants, which eventually drew crowds of devoted customers to our farm stand every week.

Adding compost is just as important if you're growing crops in pots. Food can be greedy—I mean, we're not talking about geraniums here. Fruits, vegetables, and herbs demand lots of water, sun, and nutrition, and a lively community of soil microbes is critical to helping them flower and fruit. But there's more to a good potting mix than just adding compost. Potted plants have their own unique needs, and what works for an in-ground garden won't necessarily sustain your container plants.

A GOOD POTTING MIX

The first time I shoveled garden soil into pots was pretty much the last. The organically rich soil I'd gifted my backyard plants with ended up suffocating my potted ones. Garden soil tends to be too full of clay to drain well, and can leave delicate plant roots gasping for air when it's used in a pot. Soggy soil can also lead to root rot and allow molds to flourish. I sometimes use garden soil to fill raised beds, but only after doctoring it with compost to fluff it up.

Potted plants do best in a potting mix made from materials that hold nutrients and water without the extra weight of clay. Even more important—and I can't stress this enough—it must drain well. For that reason, potting soil fashioned for container growing isn't really soil at all. Most are made with the same basic ingredients—peat for water retention, sand for weight, and vermiculite or perlite for porosity. This mixture produces an exceptional growing medium that's unlikely to turn into hard-packed soil. It's also bad for the environment.

For the eco-conscious gardener, finding the right potting mix can be challenging. Peat, which is derived from the decay of wetland plants like moss, grasses, and reeds, builds up very slowly. In fact, most peat bogs accumulate just one millimeter of peat per year, which means that, yes, the stuff we use in our potting soil took thousands of years to form. The high demand for potting soil and other peat products means that bogs are being harvested at an unsustainable rate.

Not only does mining peat destroy an important ecosystem, it has huge implications for the climate. Bogs store a significant amount of the world's organic soil carbon—about a third of it, by some estimates. Extracting and farming peat releases this carbon into the atmosphere, significantly undermining a valuable carbon sink. Perlite and vermiculite are also mined and treated with chemicals and heat to make the mineral rocks puff up like packing peanuts. The process is energy-intensive and releases a lot of greenhouse gases.

I check my potting mixes to make sure they don't contain any of these ingredients, but the truth is, most of the store-bought stuff is a mystery. Potting soil is not regulated, which means your "organic" mix can contain any of the ingredients I just described. It might also include styrofoam, bits of plastic, even unregulated sewage sludge. Most store-bought potting mixes are also sterile and devoid of microbial life. They're pumped full of synthetic nutrients to mimic the role performed by microbes in healthy soil. But any beneficial effects are fleeting because these nutrients are easily washed away.

In short, buying potting soil can be a fraught experience. Still, it's the most practical option for many of us, especially if it's hard to find the space at home to mix up your own batch. Here's how to make the most of either option.

Store-bought. Your best bet is to search for a compost-based organic potting mix certified by the Organic Materials Review Institute (OMRI). If it's hard to find, mix a bag of compost with a bag of potting mix—ideally in a one-to-one blend.

Do your research when buying compost, too. Good compost should feel a little lighter than soil. If you pick up a bag and it feels like a heavy bucket of sand, move on. And check the ingredients. Compost

POTTING MIX RECIPE

1.25 GAL. PUMICE STONE

1.25 GAL. COMPOST

2.5 GAL. COCONUT COIR

made from bark mulch and sawdust doesn't do much to feed soil microbes. The more diverse the ingredients, the healthier the soil life.

Homemade. Do-it-yourself potting mix starts with a good base made from a mixture of compost, coconut coir, and pumice stone for aeration and drainage.

To make five gallons of potting soil, combine:

A) *2.5 gallons of coconut coir.* The growing medium in this recipe is coconut coir, a natural fiber extracted from the outer husk of coconut. This green alternative to peat moss aerates your mix, allows it to drain, and holds onto moisture. It's usually sold in compressed bricks that fluff up after they've been soaked. A 1.5 pound brick is equal to just over 2.5 gallons.

B) *1.25 gallons of compost.* Compost is the champion of my homemade mixes. I tend to use my own, but you can also buy it.

C) *1.25 gallons of pumice stone.* For an airy soil structure, I use pumice, a lightweight volcanic rock. It's so light that small pieces float on water. Pumice bits create pockets of air, which promote good drainage and air circulation. While it is mined, like perlite or vermiculite, it's neither processed nor treated. You can find pumice at most garden stores in a range of sizes, from one-eighth inch to three-eighths inch. I use the smaller ones for small containers and larger grains for my bigger pots.

I mix these three ingredients in a big plastic tub and store any leftovers in a covered bin in a dry place. If you don't have the space for leftovers, simply reduce the ingredients by half or a quarter.

Soil boosts. It takes time for soil organisms to work their magic, and I cram so many plants into my pots that I like to beef up my homemade and store-bought potting mixes. Doing so can offer other benefits as well, like built-in pest control.

To boost your soil mix:

Add nutrients. One of my favorite boosters is a combination of crab meal, kelp meal, and neem seed meal. The crab meal offers a steady supply of the nitrogen, phosphorus, and calcium that plants crave and need to grow foliage, strong roots, and disease-fighting power. It's also considered a bio-pesticide because it prompts soil organisms to release special enzymes that destroy soil pests, like parasitic nematodes.

Kelp meal adds more than sixty trace minerals, along with potassium and important growth hormones. Neem seed meal, produced from a tree native to India, adds still more nitrogen and helps fight off many of the harmful soil fungi that cause disease. It also builds resistance to pests, like fungus gnats and root aphids.

ORGANIC SOIL BOOSTERS

Organic options contain a wider range of nutrients than synthetic ones, since they're made from plant and animal materials like compost, worm castings, and blood meal. They feed and support soil organisms and are gentler on plants. Synthetic fertilizers contain higher concentrations of easily-absorbed macro-nutrients, but they're inherently acidic, can kill beneficial microbes, and often contain only nitrogen, phosphorus, and potassium. Look for products certified by the Organic Materials Review Institute (OMRI). (The numbers after each fertilizer represent the ratio of nitrogen, phosphorus, and potassium. The higher the number, the more concentrated the nutrient.)

Nutrient	Symptoms of deficiency	Fertilizer
Nitrogen	Slow to zero new growth. Yellowing of older leaves.	Blood meal (12-0-0)
		Neem seed meal (6-1-2)
		Crab meal (4-3-0)
		Fish emulsion (4-1-1)
Phosphorus	Dark green or purple leaves and stems. Overall stunted growth.	Bone meal (3-15-0)
		Fish bone meal (4-12-0)
		Seabird guano (0-11-0)
		Rock phosphate (0-3-0)
Potassium	Stunted fruit development. Yellowing along leaf veins and edges. Weak stalks and immature roots.	Langbeinite (0-0-22)
		Seaweed extract (1-0-4)
		Greensand (0-0-3)
		Kelp meal (1-0-2)

Add a quarter cup of each ingredient per five-gallon batch of DIY soil, or per three-quarter cubic foot of store-bought potting mix.

Inoculate your soil. You can inoculate, or introduce specific micro-organisms into your potting mix by adding a powdered mycelium mix. This is not a true fertilizer because it has no nutritional content, but it can help jump-start plant growth. A network of mycelium, long white strings akin to fungal roots, attaches to plant roots and dramatically increases a plant's ability to absorb nutrients and water.

Another useful soil inoculant is called liquid EM-1, a naturally fermented, live microbial blend you can pour into your potting mix. The EM stands for effective microorganisms and is full of beneficial microbes naturally found in soil, like lactic acid bacteria, photosynthetic bacteria, and yeasts. It's like giving your potting mix a healthy dose of probiotics. Simply follow the instructions for best results.

Keep in mind that while the powder or liquid mix looks lifeless, it contains a mass of living organisms, so don't leave it in a hot car or outside to freeze overnight. I keep mine safe in the fridge until I'm ready to mix it.

Some experts worry about the effect of chlorinated water on the health of soil organisms. Chlorine, after all, is meant to kill unwanted microbes in our drinking supply. But microbes reproduce rapidly and, if you're also feeding your plants compost, it's highly likely their populations will rebound quickly. If you're still worried about the potential impact of chlorine, fill your watering can and leave it out overnight. The chlorine will dissipate.

Questions

How do I make my own compost indoors?

When you use a compost-based potting soil, you're supplying nutrients and building a living soil so your potted plants can thrive. But if you're an avid container gardener, chances are you don't have the outside space for a big compost bin. No worries—plenty of people have found a way to compost in their kitchens.

One option is to buy a kitchen composter, which turns food scraps into fertilizer, sometimes within twenty-four hours. These bins make the process super simple and don't take up much room. But they can be pricey, which is why many of the indoor composters I know rely on vermiculture, also known as worm composting.

All you need for a worm composter is a long, wide plastic bin (most experts recommend one cubic foot per person in your household), food scraps, and, well, worms. Any number of worm farms can ship them to you. Figure on ordering about a half pound, or roughly five hundred worms, for each cubic foot of space. Well-fed worms can double in number within about three months, so start with fewer worms, if you prefer. To set up your worm composter:

1. **Add vents.** Drill a lot of breathing holes into the lid of your bin. Place your bin anywhere the temperature hovers between 55 to 75 degrees. My friends have kept theirs in bathrooms, closets, and kitchen pantries.
2. **Make it cozy.** Soak shredded paper or cardboard for an edible bedding. Fill your container a third to halfway with the bedding.
3. **Add food.** Scatter a handful of kitchen scraps to get your worms started, and cover the food with more shredded paper. Since worms don't have teeth, add some gritty textures, like sand, cornstarch, or a bit of soil to help them efficiently break down the organic material.
4. **Add worms.** Place your worms in the bedding, tucking them into the paper material so they feel at home. Close the lid.

Let your worms settle in, and feed them every week or so. Chop up larger scraps to no bigger than two inches so they're easier to devour. Keep an eye on how quickly your worms eat; you'll want to feed them only as much as they can consume or food waste will just sit there and rot. Keep a layer of shredded paper over the top of the freshly added food scraps to ward off fruit flies.

As the worms do their work, they'll turn scraps into a type of compost called worm castings, which have the texture of tiny round balls. The compost is literal worm poo and contains all the essential nutrients plants need.

When your compost is a deep, darkish brown and moist, it's ready to go. Before removing it, feed your worms with scraps on one side of the bin for a few days so they migrate toward the new food, and you can dig out the finished compost from the other side without bothering them.

This is only a brief introduction to vermiculture. Before ordering your worms, read everything there is to know about working with them, so you know what you're in for and can give them the home they deserve.

What's good soil for a raised bed?

Sheet mulching is, hands down, my favorite way to build healthy, living soil for your raised bed. It allows you to use nutrient-dense soil

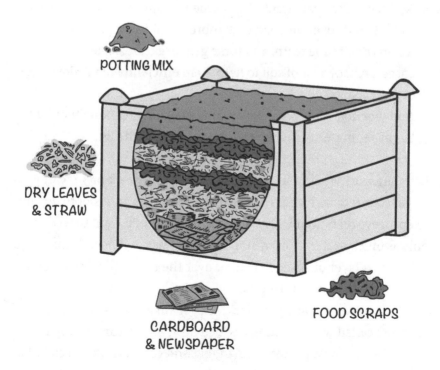

POTTING MIX

DRY LEAVES
& STRAW

CARDBOARD
& NEWSPAPER

FOOD SCRAPS

By repurposing materials usually considered waste, sheet mulching is a low-cost way to create a lot of high-quality soil.

without spending a dime. Soil rich in organic matter like compost, shredded leaves, and untreated grass clippings soaks up water and nutrients because it's statically charged. This charge holds moisture and nutrients tight so they're less likely to evaporate or drain away with frequent waterings.

Use sheet mulching with a raised bed that's at least 32 square feet in size. Smaller piles break down into compost more slowly than large ones, which generate more heat and microbial activity .

1. **Clear your planting area.** Before setting up your raised bed, mow any grass and weeds as close to the ground as possible.
2. **Lay down a barrier to discourage weed growth.** I like plain-Jane cardboard, the type without a glossy coating and free of tape or staples. It smothers weeds and eventually decomposes, adding new organic matter to the soil. Thick layers of newspaper or brown paper bags work the same way. If your planter has a built-in bottom you can skip this step, but be sure it has drainage holes.
3. **Layer on organic material.** I start by shoveling wood chips onto the cardboard weed barrier followed by untreated grass clippings and food waste, then dry leaves, cardboard, newspaper, wood chips, or straw. If you're using an elevated raised bed, skip the cardboard weed barrier and start with woodchips, and then layer on organic green materials and then brown materials. Continue this process until your raised bed is almost full, leaving about five inches of space at the top.
4. **Add a top dressing.** Fill in the remaining space with a bagged potting mix, your own homemade blend, or some finished compost (which means it has stopped decomposing) to make a nice fluffy layer in which to plant your seeds or plants. This top dressing allows you to plant crops without having to wait for the pile to break down.
5. **Water for the first season.** Water the new bed regularly if the weather is dry. Some moisture is necessary for the layers to turn into compost.

6. **Be patient.** It can take three or four months for your pile to shrink, depending on how deep your bed is and the time of year. Sheet-mulched beds decompose more quickly in the summer than in the winter.

What kinds of waste can I compost?

Here's the simple answer: anything that readily breaks down when exposed to air and water. However, all compostable materials are either nitrogen-rich or carbon-rich and to produce healthy compost, you want to aim for a 50/50 mix of each.

Nitrogen-rich materials, also known as "greens," are typically moist and include food scraps, grass clippings, coffee grounds, and more. Carbon-rich materials, or "browns," include dry stuff like wood

COMPOST MATERIALS

Material	Green/Brown	Notes
Shredded wood	Brown	Shredded wood breaks down more quickly than wood chips. Use only natural, dye-free mulch.
Dry leaves	Brown	Shred leaves so they don't mat.
Paper/cardboard	Brown	Paper towels, napkins, brown paper bags, soiled paper (pizza boxes and paper plates). Even junk mail is fine, if shredded. Tear cardboard into smaller pieces if you want it to break down more quickly.
Straw/hay	Brown	Straw generally has fewer weed seeds than hay, which makes it a better choice.
Wood chips	Brown	Chips are high in carbon so toss in only a few.
Coffee and tea	Green	Compost the grounds, filters, and tea bags.
Composted animal manure	Green	Adds beneficial bacteria.
Food scraps	Green	Fruit, veggies, eggshells, and grains are all good.
Garden waste	Green	Sort out any diseased plants. Weeds are okay, unless they've gone to seed. Use grass clippings only if they haven't been treated with herbicide. Toss in old potting soil, too.

chips, paper, straw, and leaves. If your compost is too dry or not breaking down fast enough, goose it with more greens or water. If your compost starts to stink or become slimy, add more browns.

For an indoor worm bin, browns make up the cozy bedding. Soft and shredded material, like coco coir, newspaper, and cardboard, makes the best bedding for your wriggly friends. Balance out the browns by feeding your worms nitrogen-rich kitchen scraps, including egg shells, coffee grounds, and tea bags. Note: Worms aren't fans of citrus, onions, and garlic.

When constructing a sheet-mulched raised bed, your goal is to layer on green and brown materials, lasagna-style. Brown materials might include straw, wood chips, bark mulch, leaves, paper napkins, and cardboard. Compost-worthy green materials include food waste, of course, but also animal manure, and garden waste. Old potting soil can be composted, too.

TINY REAL ESTATE OPTIONS

When I lived in the northernmost tip of the Pacific Northwest, my house was hidden under a dense canopy of towering cedar trees. Not much sun reached the lawn, so it grew in scattered patches. The only reliable light was a sliver that moved with the season. I planted tomatoes in two old wooden boxes a couple of feet across, crammed in four plants each, and leaned into that sunbeam.

That spring, the containers sat in the season's pale early light, which conveniently lit the area right outside my sliding glass door. But as the summer days lengthened and the sun shifted its path, I was forced to move my containers with it—unwittingly illustrating what

Wheelbarrow planter: I gave my aged wheelbarrow this second chance because a planter on wheels is just about the easiest way to follow the sun. The bottom was rusting so all it took to create drainage holes was a few whacks with a screwdriver and a hammer.

happens when you don't think through where to put your container garden. Those tomatoes eventually turned into a batch of mouthwatering salsa, but not before I'd moved them down the five steps outside my front door, and a couple of feet into the driveway.

Figuring out where to put your garden involves a few different calculations, but the single most important is where it's likely to get lots of light. Any sunny surface is fair game. Fruits, herbs, and vegetables need six to eight hours of direct light a day, and sun-worshippers like squash, watermelons, tomatoes, and strawberries can happily soak up ten hours or more. Plants that tolerate shade, like lettuce and arugula, can get by on fewer hours, but they need light, too. Without reliable light, you're looking at a long, slow season of spindly, weak-limbed plants.

It's not just the length of time a plant spends under light that's important. It's the quality, or intensity, of that light. South-facing plants have it made; they get the morning's first light and stay well lit throughout the day. North-facing plants aren't nearly as fortunate; they get most of their light at the end of the day when it's weakest. Eastern- and western-facing plants fall somewhere in between.

Indoor gardens face an additional challenge. While it's obvious that shades and curtains filter sun, you may not realize that even a plain glass window limits indoor light. The light diffused through glass is somewhere between 30 percent and 70 percent the strength of direct outdoor light. This is why so many indoor gardeners rely on artificial light, especially if they don't get southern light and want to grow plants through the dark winter months.

Direct light isn't an outdoor garden's only advantage. Keeping your planters outside blesses them with rain, pollinators, and easier access to industrious soil organisms. I move my plants outdoors every summer so they can soak up all those benefits. Honestly, it's just easier to grow food outside. (If you don't have that flexibility, though, no worries. I'll share steps you can take to keep an indoor food garden productive.)

To help choose the right location for your plants, ask yourself a few questions: What grows well in your region? Are you interested in

A GUIDE TO INDOOR LIGHTING

To successfully grow crops indoors, it helps to know the quality of your home's natural lighting. Whether light is low, medium, or high intensity depends on which direction it comes from, and if it's direct or indirect. Direct sunlight touches plant leaves directly, and casts hard-edged shadows. Indirect light is light that bounces off another surface before touching a plant, and creates soft shadows. Direct light exists both indoors and outdoors, but full sun indoors is only about half as strong as full sun outdoors.

Intensity	Location
Low (indirect sunlight)	While houseplants may do just fine in low-lit areas several feet away from windows, fruits, herbs, and veggies do not. If you're limited to dimly lit spaces, shine grow lights on your crops for a minimum of six hours a day.
Medium (indirect sunlight)	The indirect light of north-facing windows and shaded east- and west-facing windows may sustain shade-tolerant plants during the summer months. But it won't be enough for sun-loving plants, which will need extra light to thrive. Even shade-loving plants will appreciate supplemental light once summer is over.
High (partial direct sunlight)	Unshaded east- and west-facing windows or semi-shaded south-facing windows receive high light intensity. You can grow shade-tolerant plants year-round in this light, but sun-loving crops will benefit from grow lights when winter arrives.
Higher (full direct sunlight)	Consider yourself lucky if you have unshaded south- or southwest-facing windows. In the spring and summer months, all crops, even shade-loving ones, will grow nicely. Come fall, give sun-loving plants extra light for a successful harvest; shade-loving ones won't need it.

growing food year-round? If so, you'll have to grow food indoors at least part of the time. Do you have the room to keep plants inside, or the interest? How much of a commitment are you willing to make?

I started my first herb garden in college when I had a single windowsill, not much light, and a longing for fresh mint tea. It was a modest effort, well-suited to life as a somewhat scatterbrained student. Many years later, I'm now packing containers so full of food they amount to a miniature farm spread across my patio, kitchen, and dining room. In each instance, I had to figure out both what I wanted, and what I could manage.

For me, it's important to grow as much of my own food as I can, and I'm okay taking on the weekly, and sometimes daily, task of keeping my plants fed, watered, and well lit. If that strikes you as burdensome, consider limiting your container garden to one that lives mostly outdoors and lasts only as long as the growing season. You may appreciate the winter break.

But if you love the idea of harvesting peppers in the late fall, go for it. Indoor crops can be messy and leak water, but they're not hard to clean up after. And there's something pretty special about picking tomatoes in your kitchen. To help you work through your real estate options, let's explore a few of the more common scenarios.

Pack your patio with pots. If you've got a patio with some sun, congratulations! Even if the patio isn't south-facing, this is prime garden material. Patio crops tend to get plenty of direct sunlight, and you can use supporting walls to shelter your pots from the wind and cold. Walls absorb heat during the day and radiate it at night, which means you may be able to grow heat-loving crops like tomatoes and peppers early in the season. Patio spaces also tend to include chairs, making it easy to hang out with your plants and more likely you'll notice when they need water, some pruning, or a few bugs picked off.

Fill a windowsill. Setting up plants in a window can breathe life into a tired interior. The plants are out of the way but still very much a presence. But just because they're in the light, doesn't mean they're getting enough of it. Even herbs, about as easygoing as a plant can be, grow best in south-, west-, or east-facing windows. Northern-facing windows barely let in enough light even for shade-loving crops. If that's the only natural light you have, you'll have to supplement your crops with grow lights most of the year.

Windowsills can also get cold. In the old house where I used to live, my windows were south-facing but drafty. I ended up coating the windows with a sheet of thin plastic to protect against the chill, and my herbs got through the winter just fine. If you have a drafty sill and don't want to bother with plastic sheets, consider growing leafy greens like spinach, lettuce, and roots like carrots and beets, which can take the cold.

Start a farm in your living room. Or in your kitchen, dining room, or bedroom. I love the way my collection of plants brightens and slightly humidifies the air. Giving your plants a prominent spot indoors also means you won't forget about them! But think carefully before surrendering your space—you may find yourself wishing you could take back the place where your armchair once sat.

Crops can be demanding in other ways, too. They drop leaves, fruit, and husks, and can be a spill hazard. And do you want to cohabit with pepper pots bathed in pink, red, or blue light? The artificial lighting that's a common feature of indoor gardening often comes in rather insistent hues, though white light is also an option.

If you want to try your hand at indoor gardening, you can protect your floor or rug by placing pots on a protective mat. And you can minimize the intrusiveness of grow lights by using them only during the day and flipping them off when it gets dark, relegating crops that need the extra light to an out-of-the way corner (assuming you have one), or hiding them under a grow tent.

Raise food on the roof. I love rooftop gardens. They get plenty of light, of course, and are sizable enough to grow a decent-sized garden in big pots or even a raised container. I also know of at least two rooftop victory gardens that have brought together neighbors who wanted to grow some vegetables, and decided to share in the responsibilities.

But assuming your rooftop is a communal space, you can't just pop upstairs and plant a garden. You'll have to get permission. There's also the challenge of hauling potting mix, plants, and containers upstairs. Lugging a big watering can up and down a flight of stairs or into the elevator a few times a week is another fast way to fall out of love with a garden.

Still, if you've got access to a roof, planting a garden on it is a chance to grow lots of food, enjoy the views, and meet your neighbors—along with all the bees and other pollinators that are bound to show up.

Grow food in a greenhouse. If you'd like to keep your harvest going year round, and don't have the space, or inclination, to bring them into your kitchen or bedroom, consider doing what a friend of mine did recently, and construct a greenhouse. This is not necessarily an easy task—setting up a climate-controlled environment can be complicated and my friend eventually chose to go with a pre-made greenhouse kit. But the greenhouse has allowed her to grow cherry tomatoes, citrus trees, and herbs during Maine's ruthlessly cold springs. It also gives her more tender potted perennials a safe space to rest up over the winter. When it warms up, she just opens the flaps and lets in butterflies, beetles, and other beneficial insects.

Greenhouses come in all shapes and sizes. I rigged a tiny three-tiered greenhouse just big enough to keep five pots of early season peppers from getting too cold. If you set up a walk-in greenhouse, you can install accessories like an irrigation system, shelving units, and hanging clips for grow lights, plus stick a whole raised bed in there.

Build a raised bed. The bigger the outdoor container, the easier it is to grow food. Large gardens are more likely to harbor the healthy soil organisms that feed and support plants, and attract more of the hummingbirds and butterflies that pollinate food. It's why I recommend building a raised bed, if you can. You don't need a backyard to do it. Build one to suit whatever space you have. I've seen them in alleyways, right outside the front door of an apartment building, even in the no-man's-land between the street and sidewalk. (See "In praise of raised beds," page 65.)

Borrow a raised bed. Among the happiest gardeners I meet are those who've managed to snag space in a community garden. For people in tight spaces, it may be the only realistic way to grow food. The community gardeners I know appreciate the way it gets them outside on a regular basis to dig into the soil, meet their neighbors, and take a few deep breaths. There's a reason a number of peer-reviewed studies have found that gardening can relieve anxiety and depression, and improve our overall well being.

Community gardens also tend to have a ready supply of compost, tools, and support, plus they're a meaningful source of food for many families. For all these reasons, they're usually very popular. If you find a long wait list for a plot, consider joining an urban gardening organization working to convert more public land into green space.

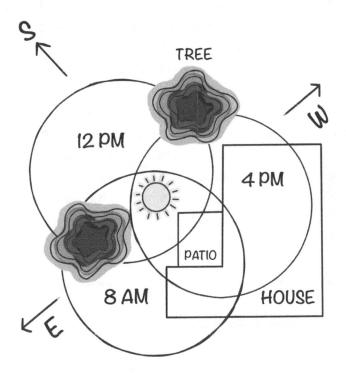

To give outdoor plants the optimum amount of sun, I recommend making a sun map. Grab some paper and a pencil and follow these simple steps: Observe your space and draw a circle around the areas where sunlight falls at 8 a.m., noon, and 4 p.m. The spot that gets the most sun is where the circles intersect. This is where you want to put your planters, if you can. Keep in mind that if it's under a tree, a sunny area in the spring will become shady in the summer.

Questions

When you raise plants in pots, does your local climate matter?

Within a week of moving back to New England, and even before I'd found a place to stay, I'd hijacked a patch of turf behind my Dad's house and mapped out a garden. As I sheet mulched the turf and prepped it with compost and wood chips, I thought about what I would plant.

At the time, I thought the fig trees I'd so loved growing in Washington would be out of the question; they'd never withstand southern Maine's harsher climate. The US Department of Agriculture (USDA) breaks the country into eleven growing zones based on the average annual minimum winter temperature in each one. My new home was in hardiness zone 6a, where temperatures can consistently fall as low as between -5 and -10 degrees.

My lament for the loss of home-grown figs lasted only until I discovered the magic of container gardening. I now wheel a potted fig tree into my house every October, and back out again in May. Container gardening allows you to more or less ignore local climate concerns if you decide to grow perennials that do well indoors, like citrus trees, pepper plants, and fig trees.

But living inside doesn't work for all perennials. Some, like blueberries, need to experience the cold in order to enter dormancy, when they pause their growth and rest before returning the following spring to fruit. So if you're growing perennials that have adapted to a particular region, and come to depend on seasonal temperature fluctuations, it's important to find crops that thrive where you live.

Things are different for annuals because there's no need to worry about their hardiness. Plant them after the last frost and harvest them before winter knocks them back. If they haven't had time to ripen, bring them inside to finish the season. They can also be planted at any time of the year indoors, regardless of the weather outside.

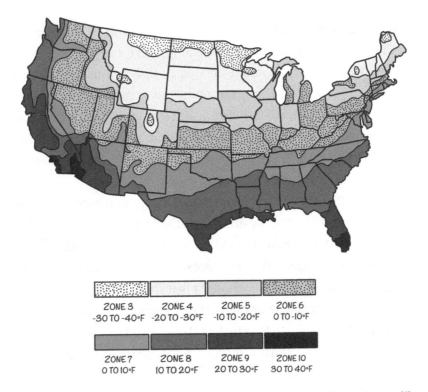

The hardiness zone map is what growers use to determine which plants are most likely to thrive in a given location. Eight of the eleven zones are in the contiguous United States. The northernmost zone is three; the southernmost is ten. Source: USDA

What should I look for in a grow light?

As a plant lover, I find it annoying that so many of the houses I've lived in have been dark. A windowless A-frame, a hidden yurt in the woods, an eighteenth-century cottage with tiny windows. Every one of them left me in a chronic state of longing for more light. This happens to plants deprived of sufficient light, too.

One spring, I potted up my early-season broccoli while waiting for the ground to thaw. After a few weeks in my spare bedroom, the plants had sprouted—and that was about it. The pale, leggy stems stretched toward the light with all they had, which wasn't enough, and they very quickly flopped over in defeat. So I did what I often do for indoor plants, and moved them under grow lights.

Plants absorb different wavelengths of light, most notably blue and red hues. Blue light encourages leaf growth, and red light, when combined with blue, encourages plants to flower. I use broad spectrum lighting, also called full spectrum lighting. While grow lights can't compare to the quality of direct sunlight, this type comes pretty close. It typically shines white from a mixture of red, blue, and green hues, making it easier on the eyes, and plants won't need supplemental sunlight, although it never hurts.

No matter the spectrum you choose, I suggest making it an LED light, which uses less energy and doesn't get too hot. I feel comfortable leaving LEDs on when I'm not home, which I can't say about many incandescent grow lights. They produce so much heat they can be a safety hazard, and scorch plants if you don't pair them with a cooling fan.

Adjust the height of your light as your plant grows; for LED lights, I like to keep them two to four inches above my plants, but it depends on the quality and intensity of your light, so refer to the product instructions for guidance.

Use a timer to make sure your seedlings are getting enough light— at least six to eight hours a day, more if you'd like to speed up the growing process. Just make sure they're also getting eight hours a day of darkness. My lights turn on when I wake up, and off when I go to bed.

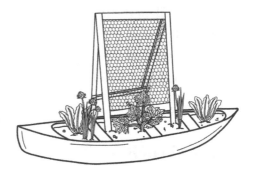

DESIGNING FOR SMALL SPACES

Before growing food in containers, I gave garden design very little thought. As a farmer, the priority was making sure my plants were well spaced and my rows reasonably straight, and that's about it. But managing for crop yields is obviously different when you're talking square inches rather than square feet, and good design is how you make it happen. It can also be key to growing healthier plants, maximizing environmental benefits, and—a recent discovery—solving home decorating challenges.

Last winter, I dragged a ladder out from under my house because I thought it might help manage the clutter of wicker baskets and terra

Canoe with trellis: When you live in Maine, it's not surprising to see the occasional abandoned boat tricked out as a planter. When I took possession of this canoe, I made the most of the space by adding a trellis. Since it was no longer lake-worthy, it drained just fine.

cotta pots piling up at the end of my dining room. I scrubbed off at least some of the rust, added some fresh blue paint, and loaded up the steps with potted plants.

In an inspired moment, I moved a deep wooden container to the foot of the ladder and filled it with scarlet runner beans, which eventually climbed all the way to the top. (So gratifying.) As an added bonus, my splendid new planter now blocks the ugly thermostat on the wall opposite my reading chair—a small, but enduring, triumph.

WORK WITH NATURE

The same pots that give you a chance to grow bumper crops of herbs, fruits, and vegetables in tight spaces allow you to support your local pollinators. In the late spring, I moved the ladder planter outside and it immediately made a stir. Butterflies flitted through my oregano, native bees zoomed around my chives, and hummingbirds were all over those scarlet runner beans.

Outdoor gardens, however small, can be a lifeline for beneficial insects and birds because pollinator-friendly habitat is shrinking. Blame agricultural sprawl, urban and suburban development, and our widespread use of pesticides. Forests and natural grasslands are being converted to grazing land at a rapid rate, thanks to our huge appetite for meat. Lawns, which cover 63,000 square miles of the lower United States, are often chemically treated, which makes a lot of that turf biological wasteland. And American farms use more than a billion pounds of pesticides every year, a number of them so toxic they've been banned by the European Union.

Since their introduction in the 1990s, a class of insecticides called neonicotinoids, or neonics, has become the most widely used class of insecticides in the world. It is considered the new DDT by many environmentalists, but a thousand times more toxic to bees. Over the past decade, the total biomass of insects has become decimated, with more than 40 percent of insect species declining and a third endangered, according to a 2019 global scientific review published in *Biological Conservation*.

It doesn't help that as plants migrate north in response to warming temperatures, they are increasingly out of sync with the bees, bugs, and butterflies that feed off them. Also suffering, the many amphibians, reptiles, fish, and birds that depend on insects for food. We do too, of course, since they pollinate the large majority of plant species, keep the soil healthy, recycle nutrients, control pests, and much more.

Container gardens create a safe place for butterflies, wasps, native bees, moths, and other pollinators to alight. They do the same for pest-eating insects, like lacewings, dragonflies, ladybugs, and spiders, which can make it easier for you to grow food without using harmful chemicals.

To attract more beneficial bugs and birds, I add plants that attract pollinators, like flowering dill, which draws in hoverflies, and the periwinkle flowers of borage, which blooms from early summer up until the first frost. I recently paired some slow-to-start cucumbers with hardy purple tansy and ended up with so many cucumbers I started dropping them off with neighbors.

I used to pull any plant that looked ready to bolt, like my cilantro. But now I leave it be. Those tiny blooms help to feed tiny pollinators. (Another plus: Allowing plants to go to seed means I don't have to replant self-sowing annuals, like arugula, cilantro, dill, and calendula, each spring.)

My other gift to pollinators is planting a variety of crops that bloom at different times so they have plenty to eat over the course of a growing season. A byproduct of all that diversity is a healthier garden.

Containers filled with different types of plants are better able to support a lively ecosystem of soil organisms and invertebrates that interact and support each other to promote soil fertility—even in pots. Along those lines, consider planting a few long-lasting perennials with your annuals; they help anchor communities of soil organisms and will add life-enhancing organic matter to the soil for years to come.

Having sworn off synthetic pesticides years ago, I rely on a number of organic pest-control solutions, a few of which involve pairing vulnerable plants with ones that can help fend off pests. I've planted chives and other aromatic herbs along with my broccoli and chard to repel leaf miners and cabbage worms. And every year I get bombarded by flea beetles, which can ruin brassica crops. I've learned to plant radishes on the far side of my deck to lure them away. The flea beetles are drawn to the decoy planting, leaving my prized broccoli and cabbage alone, and the radish roots aren't bothered by the damaged leaves left behind. (For more companion planting suggestions, see "Plants that work well together," page 45.)

If you're open to working in tandem with nature you can come up with all kinds of growing solutions. In a satisfying twist, researchers at South Dakota State University found in 2018 that farms using pesticides had ten times the insect trouble and half the profits compared to those who used organic, regenerative farming methods instead.

MAKE IT LOOK GOOD

Food gardens are usually filled with plants chosen for good taste rather than good looks. But when you're considering having them move in with you, you start thinking about them differently. Do you want a scraggly cucumber plant stretching across the floor in search of light? Or a lone broccoli plant sticking up out of a pot on your kitchen table? Why not give your plant buddies a chance to shine. You'll probably like them more, and they'll benefit from the extra attention.

My first experiment in growing a splendid-looking container farm was accidental. I planted spicy red peppers with purple basil to save space. Once the peppers appeared, the combo turned out to be so appealing I decked it with little white lights for the holidays. After

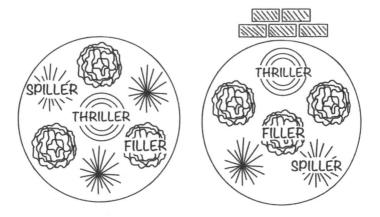

If you're looking to build beautiful and productive pots, one florist-tested approach is to include at least one thriller, up to three fillers, and two cascading spillers. If your planter is backed against a wall (right), plant your thriller in the back of the pot.

that, I started looking for more opportunities to bring out the beauty in my crops, partly because it's not all that hard to do.

You can start the way I did, by choosing colors that go well together. Planting dark purple lettuce with chartreuse arugula, for instance, can be stunning. So is pairing carrots, with their deep green, fern-like leaves, and swiss chard, with its neon yellow, red, and pink stalks. Or bright orange mini peppers with golden yellow marigolds. Sometimes the most interesting groupings are plants with the same colors, like the gorgeous purple planter I grew last summer spilling over with mauve basil, lilac-flowered chives, and plum-colored lettuce.

I'd probably have continued with my color-centric approach had I not struck up a conversation with a florist. I'd casually asked how she produces such beautiful arrangements, and she told me it was easy. Aim to thrill, fill, and spill, she said, an adage apparently every florist knows. In other words, think of your arrangement as structural, with three layers of interest. When translated to growing food in pots, it goes something like this:

- **The "thrill" is an eye-catching plant that serves as the focal point.** It's usually a plant with some height, like beans climbing a

TENT

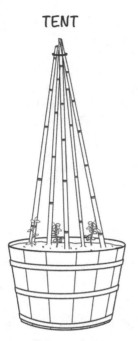

A tent trellis is best used to support climbing vines, like green beans. Just plant a few seeds at the base of each pole. It's also useful when placed as a cage over floppier plants, like tomatoes and peppers.

FENCE

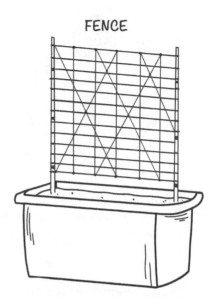

Climbers like peas and cucumbers do well with a fence trellis because their tendrils can latch on to the horizontal support. Create a fence trellis by attaching twine, wire, or fencing to sturdy stakes anchored in the soil.

A-FRAME

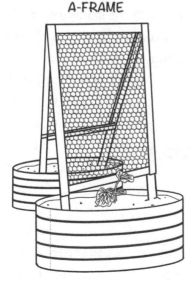

An A-frame trellis offers fairly robust support and can hold up heavier crops like cucumbers, melons, and squash. Place in one big container or in two smaller side-by-side containers. Roll out wire mesh in between the frames and secure it with staples. Start the mesh a foot from the bottom of the frame so you have room to push the feet into the soil.

trellis or a tall tomato plant. It can be an unusual color or texture, like ruffled kale or asparagus fronds. Plant it in the middle of your pot or, if your pot is against a wall, in the back to provide a dramatic backdrop.

- **The "fill" refers to shorter plants placed around your center-piece.** Covering up bare soil simply makes an arrangement look better. It also gives you another chance to pack in more plants. Classic fillers include crops like lettuce, spinach, edible flowers, and carrots.

- **"Spill" plants cascade over the sides of pots.** Think flowing strawberries, vining flowers like nasturtium, or sprawling cucumbers planted around the outside of your container and trained to flow over the edge. They help balance the vertical height of your center plant and bring some beauty of their own. (See "Crop cheat sheets," page 86, for more examples of thrillers, fillers, and spillers.)

Adopting this basic set of guidelines freed me to experiment with new plant combinations, and I found myself looking for plants I could thrust into the thriller role with the help of a trellis. I was already a fan of vertical gardening. It promotes better airflow, which helps protect plants from diseases like mildew. It offers greater access to sunlight, which makes for a more robust and longer-lasting harvest. And it now lets me promote sprawling plants, like squash, to thriller status, and grow more vegetables in tight spaces.

MAXIMIZE YOUR PLOT

The first year I succeeded in growing tomatoes well past September, I found all kinds of reasons to show them off. Friends who invited me over for dinner got used to seeing me at their doors with bowls of little cherry tomatoes. (Not to worry—I brought beer, too.) They listened to me describe the tiny farm I had at home, which kept my kitchen stocked with other staples as well, like fresh salad greens, beans, and root crops.

Maybe a few of my friends found it interesting, I don't know. But I couldn't help myself. That leap from harvesting food in the late summer to harvesting it throughout the year was profound for me. It was no accident, of course. I made it happen by adapting what I'd learned from maximizing space on our commercial farm. When you rely on growing vegetables to pay your bills, every spare patch of soil is an opportunity.

With *leave no soil bare!* as my mantra, I rely mostly on planting and harvesting annuals to fill my plate year-round. Since they mature quickly, they can produce multiple harvests in the fall, winter, and spring under the right conditions, which include a climate-controlled indoor environment, regular watering, and applying fresh seed as soon as a space opens up. One key to a year-round harvest is precision timing.

Perennials don't offer the same flexibility. Unlike annuals, they bloom and mature based on cycles cued by the sun and weather (with a few exceptions), and would prefer to stay in their pots, thank you very much, until they grow out of them. Basically, perennials ripen on their own terms, not yours. You can still team them up with annuals, which you can harvest while waiting for your perennials to flower and fruit.

Here are a few strategies for working with crops to create a successful container mini-farm.

Alternate warm- and cool-season crops. Sorting plants into cool- and warm-season plants is my favorite strategy because it invites you to grow a variety of crops, including those slow to ripen. I plant cool-season radishes in the spring, harvest them when the weather warms, and drop warm-season pepper seedlings into the spaces they leave behind. To squeak out a third crop, I introduce a cool-season plant, like lettuce, toward the end of the summer.

It's not necessary to pull out your crops for this to work. I keep my peppers around for as long as it takes for them to ripen, and tuck in other crops around their base, like a crop of cool-season carrots.

Plant crops one after the other. Planting fast-maturing annuals in succession helps you get the most out of your space. As soon as you've harvested arugula, for instance, quickly fill in the space with another scattering of fresh arugula seeds. Or switch out one crop for another. I've gotten as many as five rounds of lettuce out of a twenty-four-by-twelve-inch plastic tub in one summer, and even more once I brought it indoors for the winter. Examples of speedy annuals include lettuce, spinach, arugula, beets, carrots, and radishes.

Stagger start dates. While fast-growing plants will give you the greatest yield, it's also possible to pack in slower-growing crops like cucumbers, melons, tomatoes, peppers, and beans. I use staggered start dates to plant these crops and stretch my harvest into the fall. For tomatoes, I seed five plants every two weeks, and do this three times for a total of fifteen plants that mature at different times. This works for both outdoor and indoor growing. Stagger these heat-loving crops throughout the year and your supply will never run out, provided you have enough indoor light through the winter months.

Plant companions together. Another approach is to plant a variety of crops in your pots that get along well together, and just keep them there. This allows you to produce lots of food in one container without the hassle of switching crops in and out. It also works well for perennials.

Sympatico plants include ones that share light and water requirements, like rosemary and thyme. They may even work better together, like the way onions can fend off the cabbage looper, which is attracted to kale. I've put heat-shy lettuce plants under trellis-trained beans so they get shade in the middle of the summer. And plants don't need to be in the same pot to help each other out; I've lined up containers of sturdy berry bushes along a porch railing to create a windbreak for the tender bush beans potted just behind them.

Not all friendly plants work well in pots. I once put potatoes together with beets in a single planter, and they very quickly squeezed

EXTEND YOUR HARVEST

Unlike perennials, annuals can be planted and harvested multiple times throughout the year. Follow planting intervals to fill the harvest gaps between cut-and-come-again salad greens, for example, and eke out three rounds of squash in a season. Or grow a few crops from the cool-season column and then replace them with warm-season plants. Keep in mind that warm-season crops need plenty of time to ripen before it gets cold. Indoors, you can time your plantings on an endless loop.

Cool-season crops	Days to maturity	Planting interval
Arugula	40–60	Every two weeks
Beets	45–65	Every two weeks
Broccoli	70–90	Every four weeks
Cabbage	50–120	Every four weeks
Carrots	55–80	Every three weeks
Cauliflower	40–100	Every four weeks
Chard	50–60	Every three weeks
Cilantro	45–70	Every two weeks
Collards	50–80	Every three weeks
Garlic	90–240	Once a season
Kale	45–75	Every three weeks
Leeks	70–130	Once a season
Lettuce	30–60	Every two weeks
Onions	90–150	Once a season
Parsley	70–90	Every two weeks
Peas	50–70	Every two weeks
Potatoes	70–120	Once a season
Radishes	22–70	Every two weeks
Spinach	35–65	Every two weeks

Warm-season crops	Days to maturity	Planting interval
Basil	50–70	Every two weeks
Beans	50–90	Every two weeks
Celery	80–100	Every three weeks
Corn	60–100	Every three weeks
Cucumbers	55–70	Every three weeks
Eggplants	60–100	Every three weeks
Melons	60–100	Every three weeks
Peppers	60–100	Every two weeks
Squash	50–120	Every three weeks
Tomatoes	60–100	Every two weeks

each other out. Another miss was planting onions around the edge of a container filled with cabbage. The cabbage took off and very quickly buried my onions in deep leafy shade. By the time I'd gotten around to harvesting them, they were no bigger than golf balls. (See "Plants that work well together," page 45.)

QUESTIONS

How do you pollinate an indoor garden?

One third of all food crops need to be pollinated to produce seeds, and bees, moths, wasps, butterflies, bats, and hummingbirds share that important job. This is one of the reasons I move my house crops outside once the weather warms up.

At its most basic, successful pollination depends on carrying pollen from the anther of a flower, where it is produced, to the sticky surface of the stigma, where the fruits and seeds develop. Bees are among the most industrious pollinators and can visit up to five thousand flowers a day, swapping pollen among blooms as they search for nectar.

Attracting insect pollinators isn't necessary for all your crops. While flowers can't produce seeds without it, that's not what we're

POLLINATING NEEDS BY CROP

Self-pollinating crops have both male and female parts incorporated into their flowers and require only a slight shake or a light breeze to produce fruit indoors. Crops that are typically insect-pollinated outdoors require careful pollination by hand indoors. Use a small paintbrush or Q-tip to transfer pollen from male flower parts to female flower parts. Thankfully, there are plenty of crops you can harvest without any pollination.

Self-pollinates	Needs insect pollination	Don't need to pollinate
Beans, corn, eggplants, peas, peppers, tomatoes	Avocados, blueberries, brambles, citrus, coriander, cucumbers, melons, squash, strawberries	Arugula, basil, beets, cabbage family, carrots, celery, cilantro, lettuce, mint, onion family, oregano, parsley, potatoes, radishes, rosemary, sage, spinach, thyme

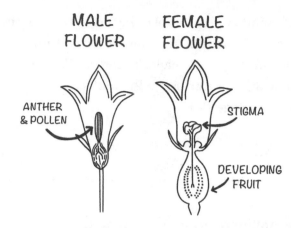

MALE FLOWER   FEMALE FLOWER

ANTHER & POLLEN

STIGMA

DEVELOPING FRUIT

Flowers have male and female parts that aid in fruit production. Complete flowers, like tomatoes and peppers, have both female and male parts in a single bloom. Incomplete flowers, like squash and cucumbers, have either male or female parts, and require hand pollination if grown indoors. The female elements are collectively called the pistil and include the stigma, which is the sticky surface meant to receive pollen. The male elements of a flower include the pollen-producing anther.

after when we grow certain crops, like salad greens, root crops, leafy herbs, cabbage, Brussels sprouts, cauliflower, broccoli, onions, and garlic. And crops like tomatoes, peppers, corn, beans, and peas have flowers that include male and female reproductive parts. Their flowers self-pollinate, shedding pollen directly onto their stigma, when physically agitated. If they're indoors, it's usually enough to just shake them a few times a week when in bloom. Or create a breeze by setting up a fan or placing plants near an open window.

For plants that rely on insects to spread pollen, like flowering fruit trees, fruiting bushes, and annual cucumbers, squash, melons, and pumpkins, you'll need to act like a bee. Use a Q-tip to snag pollen from the anther of a male blossom and spread it on the stigma of a female flower. Some crops like squash can be pollinated from the same plant while others, like most fruit trees, require cross-pollination, or at least two plants to exchange pollen.

Do this for one season and you'll gain a new appreciation for your pollinator friends, and what it would be like if they were to disappear for good.

PLANTS THAT WORK WELL TOGETHER

The practice of companion planting can help deter pests, attract beneficial insects, improve soil fertility, increase yields, and create a thriving, biodiverse garden. However, the rules aren't cut-and-dried and most evidence is anecdotal. Start with these suggested pairings, but then experiment for yourself and observe your results. In general, aim to pair up plants with similar light requirements, but different rooting depths so they don't compete for water and nutrients (shallow = 6–12 inches, medium = 12–18 inches, deep = 18+ inches). Check out the pollination notes to ensure a successful harvest, both indoors and outdoors. (See "How do you pollinate an indoor garden?" page 43.)

Crop	Root depth	Light needs	Companion plantings
Avocados	Medium	Full sun	Boost fruit production by growing near pollinator magnets like calendula, marigold, and nasturtium. Plant companions in separate pots to prevent competition for space, light, and nutrients.
Basil	Shallow	Full sun	Both annual and perennial basil protect tomatoes from hornworms and thrive among all other crops.
Beets	Medium	Full sun to partial shade	Plant beets among tall, warm-season crops like tomatoes, pole beans, and peppers. Beets appreciate the shade in hot weather. Other neighborly plants include cool-season crops like lettuce, kale, and cabbage as well as pest-repelling onion and garlic.
Brambles: blackberries, raspberries	Deep	Full sun	In separate pots nearby, grow flowering plants to encourage pollination and aromatic herbs to deter pests. Brambles also provide an excellent windbreak for tender seedlings and crops.
Blueberries	Medium	Full sun	More pollination means more fruit, so grow pollinator magnets like calendula, marigold, and nasturtium in separate, adjacent pots.
Bush Beans	Medium	Full sun	Plant this nitrogen-fixing crop next to heavy feeders, like tomatoes and members of the cabbage family, to keep them happy. Don't plant beans next to garlic; alliums can inhibit their growth.
Cabbage family: cabbage, kale, collards, broccoli, cauliflower	Medium	Full sun to partial shade	Cabbage loopers and worms may attack your brassicas, so plant them with pest-repelling companions like mint, nasturtium, rosemary, sage, oregano, thyme, and all members of the onion family.

Crop	Root depth	Light needs	Companion plantings
Calendula	Shallow	Full sun to partial shade	Plant this flowering medicinal herb everywhere to deter pests and attract pollinators.
Carrots	Medium	Full sun to partial shade	Carrot companions include beans, leeks, lettuce, onions, garlic, peas, peppers, and any member of the cabbage family. Do not plant carrots with dill, which can attract the carrot rust fly.
Celery	Shallow	Full sun to partial shade	Grow celery near the cabbage family to repel cabbage worms, and near cucumbers to repel whiteflies. Planting members of the onion family nearby may enhance the sweetness of celery.
Chard	Medium	Full sun to partial shade	This cool-weather crop grows well with everything. Protect chard from the heat by growing it in the shadow of tall crops like corn, pole beans, peppers, and tomatoes.
Cilantro	Shallow	Full sun	Sympatico with everything. This fragrant herb repels aphids and attracts beneficial insects with its blooms.
Citrus	Deep	Full sun	Fruit trees benefit from neighboring aromatic herbs that repel pests, as well as from pollinator magnets like borage and bee balm that aid in fruit production. Plant companions in separate pots to avoid competition.
Corn	Medium	Full sun	In the classic three sisters planting, peas and beans climb up corn, while fixing nitrogen in the soil. Other companions include cucumbers, squash, and melons, which like to grow under corn's shade.
Cucumbers	Medium	Full sun	Plant with pollinator magnets for a bigger harvest. Cucumbers do well at the base of crops like tomatoes, peppers, and corn. In return, this sprawling crop suppresses weeds and acts as a living mulch.
Eggplants	Medium	Full sun	Gets along with other sun-loving nightshades like tomatoes and peppers. Plant with pest-repelling neighbors like nasturtiums, onions, garlic, and aromatic herbs.
Lettuce	Shallow	Full sun to partial shade	Plant this cool-season crop underneath tall warm-season crops, like pole beans, for much needed shade in hot weather.

Crop	Root depth	Light needs	Companion plantings
Marigolds	Shallow	Full sun to partial shade	Repels nasty root nematodes, but only after the plant has matured and the roots are left to decompose in the soil. Beloved by pollinators.
Melons	Medium	Full sun	Plant flowers like asters, zinnias, and calendula nearby to boost fruit production. Plant small, fast-maturing crops like radishes and lettuce among your melons and harvest them before they're shaded out.
Mint	Shallow	Full sun to partial shade	Mint is an aggressive spreader, so plant it in its own pot. This aromatic herb deters cabbage moths and ants.
Nasturtiums	Shallow	Full sun to partial shade	An aphid and cabbage looper magnet; use nasturtiums as a sacrifcial crop. Pollinators love it, too.
Onion family: onions, garlic, scallions, shallots, leeks, and chives	Shallow	Full sun	Thanks to their strong odor, plants in the onion family repel pests like aphids, cabbage loopers, beetles, slugs and snails, rabbits, and more. Scatter them throughout your garden, but never in the same pot as beans and peas.
Oregano	Shallow	Full sun	Oregano's strong aroma effectively deters pests and its flowers attract aphid predators. Plant with other drought-tolerant herbs like rosemary and sage.
Parsley	Shallow	Full sun to partial shade	This herb gets along with every plant and attracts beneficial insects for natural pest control.
Peas	Medium	Full sun	Use this nitrogen-fixer as a first succession crop, following with heavy feeders like tomatoes, peppers, or any member of the cabbage family. Do not sow seeds next to onions and garlic, which can inhibit germination.
Peppers	Medium	Full sun	Plant peppers among shade-tolerant leafy greens that will cover soil and suppress weeds in return. Tomatoes, eggplants, and aromatic herbs also thrive as companions.
Pole beans	Medium	Full sun	Part of the classic trifecta: corn, beans, and squash. Beans fix nitrogen and use corn for vertical support. Pole beans can share a trellis with peas, tomatoes, or cucumbers, and a pot with shade-tolerant crops like beets, radishes, lettuce, and celery. Do not plant among onions or garlic.

Crop	Root depth	Light needs	Companion plantings
Potatoes	Medium	Full sun to partial shade	This mostly underground plant pairs well with shallow-rooted veggies and herbs like kale, leeks, chives, and cilantro. Nitrogen-fixing beans make a great soil-enhancing neighbor, and potatoes repel the Mexican bean beetle in return.
Radishes	Shallow	Full sun to partial shade	Tuck in radishes among melons, cucumbers, squash, and eggplant starts. Then harvest this fast-maturing crop before it's shaded out. Radishes get along well with all cool-season veggies and herbs. Plus, you can use this crop as a trap for aphids and flea beetles, which will attack the foliage but not the roots you're after.
Rosemary	Medium	Full sun	Plant near members of the cabbage family to deter the cabbage moth. Repels bean beetles and carrot flies, too. Rosemary prefers the company of other dry-loving herbs like oregano and sage.
Sage	Shallow	Full sun	Plant near cabbage-family plants and radishes to stave off the cabbage moth. Gets along well with rosemary and oregano.
Spinach	Shallow	Full sun to partial shade	Plant this cool-season crop in the shade of warm-season crops, like tomatoes and peppers, or with other salad greens.
Squash	Deep	Full sun	Its large leaves act like a living mulch. Grow any quick-maturing crops, like radishes and lettuce, in between squash plants before they get too big. Plant it with nasturtiums to repel squash bugs.
Strawberries	Shallow	Full sun	Plant strawberries with lettuce and spinach to encourage more growth from all three plants. The leafy greens may also hide ripening berries from birds. Other friends include garlic, onions, herbs, and marigolds.
Thyme	Shallow	Full sun	Plant near members of the cabbage family to deter the cabbage moth. Grows well with everything and attracts pollinators, too.
Tomatoes	Deep	Full sun	Plant with basil and dill, to protect against hornworms. Basil may make your tomatoes taste better. Other companions include marigolds, peppers, and aromatic herbs.

CONTAINER GARDEN RECIPES

Last year, when I planted spring greens and beets, I surround-ed them with perennial chives to help repel pests and yellow yar-row to attract beneficial insects. When they were ready to harvest, I had summer crops, including eggplant and bush beans, all lined up and ready to be planted in their place. With a little planning, that one pot yielded a healthy supply of food, and kept a swarm of pollinators happy, all season long.

Growing more than one crop in a planter can be as simple as team-ing up lettuce and carrots, or tucking in some basil around the bottom of a tomato plant. But if you're up for producing as much food as you can in a way that looks good and makes your corner of the world a bit

Half-barrel with squash: A whiskey barrel offers depth, which makes it a good option for deep-rooted plants. One drawback is how heavy it can be, so make sure you're happy with where you put it.

more eco-friendly, aim to batch three, four, or six different vegetables in a single pot.

It took me a while to pull this off—and I'm familiar with the preferences of different plants. So to help get you started, and maybe spare you some pain, I'm sharing a few of my favorite container recipes—ones that look good, encourage resilience, and help you get the most out of your small plot.

Every one of the following combinations can be grown indoors or outdoors. With indoor gardens, start them any time of the year. With outdoor ones, plant them after the last spring frost. If you're ambitious and decide to plant all the recipes at once, they will blossom at different times so you can give visiting pollinators plenty to feed on.

Each of these tiny gardens can be planted in one big pot. If that's too bulky for your space, it's okay to break out any combination of the ingredients into smaller containers. Clustering the smaller planters will still look good, because I've chosen these combinations in part for their looks. And you'll attract more pollinators than you would with the plants on their own. If you're working with a spacious raised bed, consider filling it out with more than one recipe so you get a greater variety of crops.

I've offered fairly precise instructions and amounts because I want to make these easy for you to follow. But they're meant to be

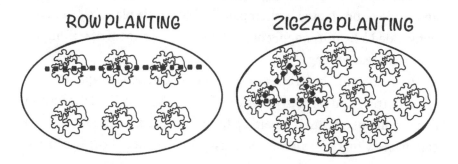

The simplest way to create more space in your planter is to plant your seeds or starts in a staggered or zigzag pattern. This allows for more plants, and gives them the room they need to mature.

tinkered with, so please do experiment. As in any recipe, just double the quantity if you have the space.

TINY HERB GARDEN

Herbs are small and resilient plants, which make them a good low-maintenance option. This particular collection of perennial herbs is also beautiful, thanks largely to purple chive flowers and lavender-tinged sage leaves. They're companionable because they all like full sun and share the same water requirements, unlike thirstier herbs like basil and parsley. When grown indoors, they'll produce fresh sprigs to clip all winter long. Outside, they'll attract pollinators and deter some pests, which is why I keep a cluster of potted herbs at the base of my larger salad containers.

Pots: Use a single planter at least two feet wide, or spread out the plants among a few containers.

Plants: Use starts (baby plants).

>   *Thrill*: Hill hardy or Arp rosemary, cold hardy (one start)
>   *Fill*: Onion or garlic chives (two starts)
>   Tri-color sage (two starts)
>   *Spill*: Marjoram or oregano (two starts)
>   Lemon thyme (two starts)

Planting tips: Most perennial herbs can take up to four weeks or more to sprout. So I prefer picking up plants from a garden center or starting my own seedlings indoors during the winter. They need eight hours of direct sunlight to thrive, so use artificial light if growing indoors in low-light conditions.

Plant your rosemary in the center of your pot and place the chives and sage around it in an alternating pattern. Aim to space your herbs

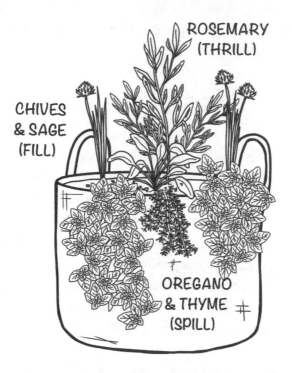

ROSEMARY
(THRILL)

CHIVES
& SAGE
(FILL)

OREGANO
& THYME
(SPILL)

six to eight inches apart. If you can't find a big enough container, it's fine to move them closer. Plant the thyme and marjoram around the edges of the container, so they can spill over the sides and open up more space for the rosemary, chives, and sage.

Indoor/outdoor: If your garden lives indoors, move it outdoors in the late spring to help feed the neighborhood population of pollinators, which love to drink from these aromatic plants. Or swap in some hardier oregano for the marjoram, and keep it outdoors year-round.

Upkeep: Prune your herbs every spring to keep the garden compact, or move it into a bigger pot every other year. Clipping blooms as they appear helps keep your herbs tasting fresh; otherwise they can turn bitter. I tend to sacrifice a few plants to attract pollinators.

Harvest: Snip sprigs of herbs as needed. To minimize stress, avoid removing more than one third of the plant at a time.

SUPER SALAD MIX

This mixed greens planter is so fast-growing it's usually ready to harvest within six weeks. It's also beautiful, thanks to rich bands of purple and green lettuces mixed in with edible, peppery orange, yellow, or red nasturtiums, and yellow-orange calendula. The calendula is a popular attraction for pollinators like native bumblebees, and its foliage provides some shelter for pest-eating bugs, like lacewings.

Pots: Use one pot at least eighteen inches wide, or two pots if you want the full benefit of succession planting and an uninterrupted harvest.

Plants: To make this cool-season mix work, I recommend using both seeds and starts.

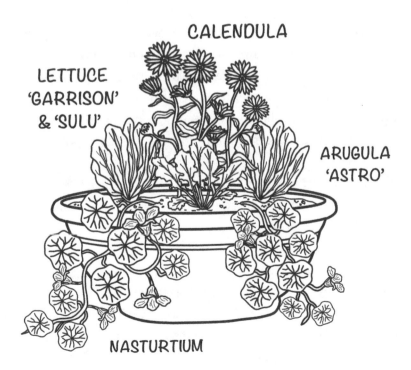

CALENDULA

LETTUCE
'GARRISON'
& 'SULU'

ARUGULA
'ASTRO'

NASTURTIUM

The following amounts are for one container.

> *Thrill:* Calendula (one start)
>   *Fill:* Garrison purple loose leaf lettuce, mildew resistant
>   (one-half seed packet)
>   Sulu green loose leaf lettuce (one-half seed packet)
>   Astro arugula (one-half seed packet)
> *Spill:* Nasturtiums, any variety of colors (two starts)

Planting tips: Plant the calendula in the center of your pot. Next, scatter your lettuce seeds in thick bands on either side, alternating the purple and green. Lightly scatter the arugula seeds in the remaining space in front of the calendula. (Thin the seedlings to about a half inch apart after they sprout.) Add both nasturtium starts to the front of the planter, framing the calendula on either side. If you'd like to keep your harvest going, wait two or three weeks before planting your second container in the same way.

Indoor/outdoor: This cool-season mix grows best in the fall and spring, but you can keep it going through the summer if you move it into shade, and give it plenty of water. Since most leafy greens don't require much direct sunlight, they're easier to grow inside than many other garden annuals, and it's possible to plant multiple rounds all year. Another plus: When grown indoors, this mix does not need to be pollinated.

Upkeep: The best way to maintain this garden is by harvesting it frequently. The calendula will produce more flowers if you deadhead, or pinch off, the spent flowers.

Harvest: The more greens you pick, the more they'll grow. Harvest your greens by picking individual leaves across the mix all season long, or cut the loose heads down to about two inches high and allow them to grow back. Salad greens like these are what vegetable farmers call a cut-and-come-again crop.

SALSA FRESCA

This arrangement is a sweet combination of acid and heat, and it's beautiful. Tomatoes and spicy peppers are tender perennials, which means they can live through the winter when given enough warmth and light. Add a few easy-to-grow shallots and a slow-to-bolt cilantro plant, and you have the ingredients you need to grow your own salsa. The addition of sweet alyssum invites visits from beneficial insects like hoverflies, which protect your garden by feasting on pests like aphids and leafhoppers.

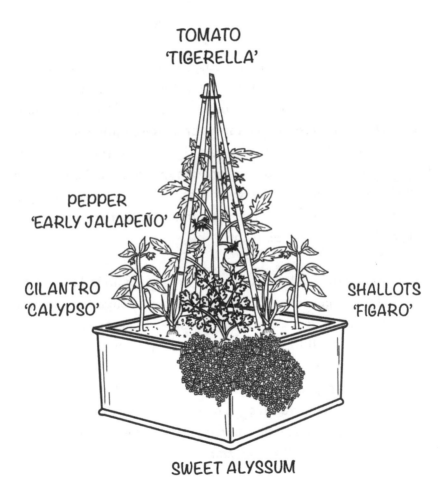

TOMATO
'TIGERELLA'

PEPPER
'EARLY JALAPEÑO'

CILANTRO
'CALYPSO'

SHALLOTS
'FIGARO'

SWEET ALYSSUM

Pots: Choose a container at least two feet by two feet wide or twenty-four inches in diameter.

Plants: This combination grows best from starts since it takes a while for the fruits to ripen.

> *Thrill*: Tigerella vining tomato (one start)
> *Fill*: Early jalapeño or, for more kick,
> serrano peppers (two starts)
> Figaro shallots (six starts)
> Calypso cilantro (one start)
> *Spill*: Sweet alyssum, any color
> (three starts)

Planting tips: Plant your tomato in the back center of your pot to create an eye-catching backdrop, and place it under a tent trellis so the vines can climb it. On either side of the tomato, plant a pepper, preferably a foot away. Place the cilantro start in the empty space directly in front of your tomato plant, at least eight inches from the base of the plant. Scatter the shallots, using a zigzag pattern, in between the peppers and cilantro. Add the sweet alyssum plants around the edges of your planter. They'll spill over and, thanks to shallow roots, leave plenty of space for the other plants.

Indoor/outdoor: You'll need to replant the shallots and cilantro each year. But spicy peppers and tomatoes will last through the winter if you bring them indoors. Bring them inside in late August or early September. Once all the fruit has ripened, prune back most of the growth and let your plants rest.

Move your peppers and tomatoes back outside in the spring when nighttime temperatures warm to 55 degrees, so they can start to put on new growth and be pollinated. If you don't want to bother keeping them indoors all winter, start from scratch with fresh plants in the spring.

Upkeep: This container is relatively low-maintenance. To keep your tomato from taking over the pot, secure its vines to the trellis as it grows. Peppers sometimes benefit from getting extra support, too. If your plant starts to flop over with the weight of all those peppers, secure it to a sturdy bamboo stake.

Harvest: The cilantro will be ready to harvest first. Clip its leaves as needed. I've chosen a heat-resistant variety to help reduce this plant's tendency to bolt in hot weather. The shallots, tomatoes, and peppers will mature three to four weeks later.

BEANS, BEES, AND BUTTERFLIES

This mix is truly striking thanks to towering, trellis-trained scarlet runner beans, a perennial with fiery red blooms that is irresistible to pollinating birds and insects. The marigolds lend more color and help keep away pests, specifically the Mexican bean beetle, which would devour the runner beans if left unchecked. The arrangement includes a dense planting of feathery carrot greens and flowing cucumber vines topped with yellow flowers that grow into round, baseball-sized fruits.

Pot: Pick a thirty-inch-wide pot or, if you love carrots and need more room, aim for a three-by-three-foot container. You can also opt for a smaller pot and plant the beans in their own container, at least eighteen inches wide.

Plants: These are best grown from seeds, except for the marigold starts, which supply a splash of color while you wait for your veggies to grow in.

> *Thrill:* Scarlet runner beans (up to six seeds)
> *Fill:* Danvers carrots (one seed packet)
> Marigolds, any variety (four starts)
> *Spill:* Lemon ball cucumbers (four seeds)

Planting tips: Build a tent trellis for the beans and plant one or two bean seeds per leg. Scatter half your carrot seeds in a circle around the trellis. Avoid putting seeds within the trellis footprint because once the beans take off, any carrots inside the base of the trellis will be shaded out. Once your seeds sprout, thin out the seedlings so they're one or two inches apart.

Place your cucumbers on either side of your bean plant, about three inches away from it. Once they start growing, gently coax them over the edge so they spill over rather than take up valuable space.

Indoor/outdoor: If you live in a frost-free climate, you can leave your planter outdoors over the winter. Otherwise, move it indoors in the fall—though it can be a little awkward thanks to the towering beans. If you choose to grow this planter indoors, you'll need a grow light and have to manually pollinate your beans and cucumbers.

Upkeep: Beans, carrots, and cucumbers are carefree crops and grow without much attention. If you plan on keeping your beans outside over the winter, remove any old cucumber vines, harvest the remaining carrots, and cover your planter with mulch. Scarlet runner beans are perennial and sprout from tuberous roots, so you won't have to replant them the following season. In cold climates it's possible to harvest the root tubers by snipping off pieces for safekeeping indoors, storing them in a cool, dry place, and planting them again the following spring.

Harvest: Picking beans constantly will cue your plant to produce more. Enjoy them as green beans or let the seeds plump up inside the pods for a meaty shelling bean. Pull your carrots any time. Your cucumbers may start off a little slow, but once they start producing, you'll be picking them at least once a week. Keep at it if you want to keep them coming.

POTS & PLANTERS

Take one look at the pile-up of mismatched containers on my porch, and you'll have a sense of my priorities when it comes to containers. I lean toward cheap, available, and functional. Over the years, I have repurposed rusty watering cans, busted wheelbarrows, leftover easter baskets, decorative buckets, cast-iron bathtubs, a landlocked canoe, cinder blocks, hollow tree stumps, and even dresser drawers.

I share my love of jury-rigged planters to suggest the range of options available, but also to remind you that a container's job is simple: It needs to hold potting mix and include drainage holes, so your plant stays hydrated without drowning.

Many people choose their pots for looks, which is understandable given the intimate nature of container gardening. They're part of

Cement block with strawberries: A couple of summers ago, I planted strawberries in a row of cinder blocks because they retain warmth, which berries love. The open bottom also invites healthy soil organisms. My berries flourished.

your daily life, often in close quarters, and it's important that you like the way they look! My collection of misfit pots aside, my own taste has evolved as my indoor garden has grown. I recently upgraded the old bucket in my living room to a vintage cerulean blue pot now overflowing with strawberries. *I love it.*

It is possible to choose the wrong pot. If the container is too small, a top-heavy plant can topple over and its roots become bound up, stunting its growth. If the pot is too roomy, it can set up your plants for mold and root rot because without roots extensive enough to suck up water, potting mix takes longer to dry out. A poor-fitting pot is not a big problem for annuals, which don't stick around for very long. But perennials do best cradled in closely fitted pots, with no more than two inches of soil around their root ball.

The container you choose can determine how much watering your plant needs, and whether it can withstand climate extremes.

UNDEVELOPED ROOTS
CREATE SOGGY
CONDITIONS

HEALTHY ROOTS
SUCK UP WATER
FASTER

DRAINAGE HOLES SATURATED SOIL

A small perennial living in a pot that's too big (left) may suffer from root rot and mold issues. Even with drainage holes, potting mix can stay moist for too long if the plant is undeveloped and the pot so roomy it's hard for roots to suck up much water. To prevent this from happening, plant perennials in pots with just enough room for roots to stretch out.

POTS & PLANTERS

Worth noting: I've become more careful about reusing pots that come with a history. I should never have used an old cement bird bath, for instance, because of the likelihood it contained asbestos, which was often used as an additive in cement mixtures between 1940 and the 1980s. That pretty red container you find in a secondhand store may contain lead paint. Residual agricultural chemicals, gasoline, or other toxins can linger in any type of recycled bucket. In short, if you don't know the history of your secondhand container, you're better off finding a new one.

POROUS CONTAINERS

Porous containers like terra cotta, fabric, and concrete allow potting mix to breathe. By drawing out excess water, they help create pockets of air, which prevent even the fluffiest mix from becoming hard-packed and make it easier for soil organisms to breathe and thrive. These gaps also allow hot air to escape.

If you're trying to cultivate a potting mix that works like living soil, a porous pot is the way to go. They can be fragile, and potting soil tends to dry out more quickly, which can lead to plant stress, particularly for crops like melons and mint that prefer moist conditions. But there's an easy solution: regular watering.

Concrete or cement. Cement is an ingredient in concrete, which can also contain sand and gravel. Both are rugged enough to make them good long-term choices for tiny victory gardens, and are available in endless shapes and sizes.

Pros: Won't tip over in windy spaces. Outlasts most other pots. Color and design is baked in so it never fades. Can absorb and radiate heat, which protects roots against frost and buffers plants against weather extremes.

Cons: Big containers are heavy and hard to move around; place big pots on wheels, if you can. Relatively expensive compared to other materials. A single drainage hole for large planters is usually inadequate; with these materials, it's hard to add more holes. Can crack or break if left outside in the winter. At the end of the growing season, move it indoors, or wrap it in a blanket or some other form of insulation.

Fabric grow bags. Fabric bags are typically made from a thick and breathable material similar to what's used in reusable grocery bags. While not the most attractive option, they can prevent plants from becoming root-bound; when a plant's roots grow near the edge of the bag, the exposure to air limits their growth. I recommend these for gardeners who rent their homes and want an easy way to pack up their garden when they leave.

Pros: Come in a range in sizes, from one gallon to two hundred gallons. Can be planted in the ground, if you have the space, because most are biodegradable. Very light and easy to fold and store when not in use.

Cons: Not as durable as other materials; may need to be replaced every couple of years. Soft walls make the pouches vulnerable to falling over if packed with top-heavy plants, like vining beans or big tomatoes. More expensive compared to other longer-lasting materials.

Unglazed terra cotta. Terra cotta, a name that means "baked earth" in Italian, is clay-based earthenware, looks as good as it sounds, and is affordable. Those features, coupled with its porosity, make this material my favorite. Note: Glazed terra cotta or ceramic pots are nonporous and behave more like plastic pots.

Pros: The production process does not include any harmful chemicals or elements. (But it's neither biodegradable nor recyclable.) Pot sizes are standardized, unlike plastic pots.

Cons: Large pots are heavy and hard to move around on your own, or without a plant trolley. Lime and mineral salts can stain your pots, though they're easy to clean with a little scrubbing. Can crack in freezing temperatures. Before it gets cold, either bring your pots inside or wrap them in something warm.

Wooden boxes. It's easy to build raised beds with wood. I also happen to like the way a wooden planter looks. Choose wood that's resistant to rotting, like cedar. Avoid using pressure-treated lumber, which contains harmful chemical preservatives.

Pros: Insulates plants against summer heat. Affordable and flexible enough to customize and build to fit. Among the only porous materials that does not dry out quickly.

Cons: Bottoms will rot with too much moisture; line wooden planters with plastic, or porous landscape fabric. Wood splits with age, and nails can rust and weaken. Protect your wood with water-based paint or stain or, for a chemical-free treatment, use linseed oil. Ants and other wood-loving pests are happy to move right in.

NONPOROUS CONTAINERS

Plastic, metal, and fiberglass containers are nonporous, which means they don't breathe well and can't support soil organisms as easily. They lock in moisture and ease watering demands, but are easy to overwater. That said, these containers can be among the most affordable and versatile.

Fiberglass. Fiberglass is made from thin fibers of spun glass held together by resin. It can be made to mimic popular materials, like stone, terra cotta, or ceramic, but is lightweight, which makes it good for hauling plants indoors and outdoors, and for stocking rooftop gardens.

Pros: Lightweight and easy to move around. Rust-proof and weather-resistant. It won't crack from freezing or thawing. Affordable and long-lasting.

Cons: Can be too lightweight for tall crops that need trellising; the added vertical weight can topple planters not fastened to the ground. Traps high summer heat, which can cook plant roots; if you live in a desert zone, keep these pots in a shaded area. Quality matters; the cheap stuff can quickly lose shape and even melt, or become brittle and break.

Galvanized steel. This metal is durable, and the troughs make attractive planters. But metal heats up and freezes easily, which can lead to dangerously hot or cold soil and harm plants. Perennials grown in metal pots often don't make it through the winter.

Pros: Attractive. Retains moisture for crops that need it. Affordable in large sizes, including raised beds.

Cons: Steel is highly susceptible to temperature change; it can freeze plants and get hot enough to cook roots. This planter is best kept in shaded areas or indoors. It's easy to overwater, especially if kept indoors; there's some concern that small amounts of zinc and cadmium can leach into soil over time, but it's unlikely to present a safety concern.

Plastic. Plastic containers come in a wide variety of shapes, colors, and sizes, and are cheap, which makes them a popular choice. Thick plastic is durable and easy to reuse. Some plastics do leach toxins when exposed to heat or damaged, but only in very small amounts. To limit any risk, choose plastic materials with the numbers 1, 2, 4, or 5. Most nursery plastic containers are code 5.

Pros: Lightweight and easy to move around. Thick plastic can last for years. Easy to sterilize with boiling water or disinfectant sprays, so you can reuse.

POTS & PLANTERS

Cons: Can tip over in windy areas, and even blow away. Cheap plastic can become brittle and break when exposed to cold temperatures or lots of sun. Often ends up as waste in landfills because they're almost impossible to recycle.

IN PRAISE OF RAISED BEDS

Two years ago, a friend in Santa Cruz, California, asked for my help bringing to life a hard and rocky backyard. I asked him what he wanted to grow. "Everything!" he told me. He could have built fresh, fertile soil through the process of sheet mulching. (See "What's good soil for a raised bed?" page 18.) But he didn't want to wait, plus he needed a garden that would work long term for his aging parents, one that minimized bending and kneeling. So we came up with another plan.

My friend built three spacious four-by-eight-foot raised beds, each standing three feet high. He then planted a variety of vegetables, squash and cucumbers among them. In his very first season, he harvested bushels of cherry tomatoes, more cucumbers than he could pickle, and enough greens that he stopped buying them. His biggest gardening problem was figuring out how to deal with his enormous bumper crop of squash, since he'd run out of ways to cook it.

Raised beds are easier to maintain than smaller pots because they don't dry out as quickly in the heat. The larger mass of soil makes it easier for plants to cope with freeze and thaw cycles that could otherwise uproot them and shatter pots. In a larger bed, you're more likely to keep living soil alive from one year to the next. Raised beds also drain better, and there's less danger of root rot during rainy periods. On the downside, if your plants struggle with disease for more than one season, you'll have to empty out the soil—a lot of it—and replace it with fresh stuff. Or solarize the infected soil by covering it with a clear or black plastic tarp for four to six weeks.

A raised garden bed is either built on legs, or open-bottomed and lined with cardboard to block weeds. Not only can it help gardeners bypass rocky or poor soil, it's simply the most efficient way to grow food in containers, and a key reason many of the country's community gardens are so bountiful. When built directly on the ground, it invites worms, bacteria, and fungi that already populate the soil. But even a bed built off the ground can become part of the outdoor ecosystem, assuming you feed it with compost.

To fill your raised bed, you can use potting mix—though that can be cost prohibitive. Or you can create your own living soil by sheet mulching if your bed is big enough or by using a 50/50 blend of garden soil mixed with compost.

There's no right or wrong size for a raised bed, although a convenient width is between three and four feet—wide enough to reach across without having to climb into it. Build your bed as long as you want and at least a foot deep so the roots have plenty of underground space. Cut your own pieces to assemble, or rely on any number of precut kits that come in wood or metal. They're fairly easy to take apart if you want to take them with you to your next home.

If you're trying to decide whether to build one on the ground or off the ground, you might want to test your soil first. Contaminated soil is, unfortunately, a fairly common problem, especially in land located near industrial activity, high-traffic areas, or agricultural zones. Substances like pesticides, lead, arsenic, asbestos, and polycyclic aromatic hydrocarbons (toxic chemicals released by burning coal, oil, gas, garbage, or tobacco) are among the most common pollutants.

A simple soil test analyzed by a local lab can tell you whether or not your soil is contaminated. If it is, don't lose heart; either build your bed on legs, or make the barrier between the ground and your fresh soil extra thick. You can also build your beds tall, the way my friend did, to prevent roots from coming in contact with toxins. For annuals, most roots don't extend beyond two feet deep. Perennials, on the other hand, can root to depths of four feet or more for trees and shrubs, so they might not be the best choice if you're building over contaminated soil.

Those new raised beds in my California friend's backyard turned out to be life-changing. When we last spoke, he told me he's going back to school to study agriculture, with plans to start his own neighborhood farm. Honestly, most of the people I know who've tried growing food fall in love with it. Here's hoping it happens for you, too.

QUESTIONS

How do I make sure my pots drain properly?

The most important feature to consider in a container is whether it includes holes that allow water to escape so your plants don't drown. If you have a clay, concrete, cement, wooden, or ceramic pot that doesn't include any holes—like the sturdy teapot I once filled with a doomed basil plant—you can drill holes with a high-speed electric drill and a half-inch drill bit. Plastic pots are obviously easier—just punch in holes with a screwdriver.

Aim to include at least one drainage hole for a small to medium pot. For large pots, include four to six holes. You really can't have too many.

If you notice your pots are draining poorly, despite plenty of holes and a good potting mix, check the bottoms to make sure they're clear of debris. Placing pots directly on the ground or on top of a beautifully crafted saucer can also block drainage holes. I get around this by placing my pots on small feet, such as equal-sized rocks or slim pieces of wood, to create a gap. Or just drill a few holes in the sides of your container at the base.

If you're using a decorative pot without any drainage, I recommend using the pot-inside-a-pot technique. Fill the base of your outer, more decorative pot with gravel before slipping in your liner pot, complete with drainage holes. The gravel base elevates your liner pot so that any excess water has a place to go after a deep watering. This is also a good design feature if you want to protect indoor surfaces from water damage.

SIZING UP A POT

The only complicated thing about pots is the lack of standardization. A four-gallon container can come in a variety of shapes and several combinations of width and height. "Standard" nursery pots labeled five gallons or seven gallons actually hold around four gallons and five gallons of potting mix, respectively. I suggest you forget about volume labels and choose a pot that looks deep enough to accommodate the roots, and wide enough to fit mature plants. Then see how it goes. Worst case, you have to move your plants into a new pot.

1–4 inches deep (½–2 pints)	Seedlings
4–6 inches deep (1–3 quarts)	Seedlings, young transplants
6–8 inches deep (1–2 gallons)	Arugula, leeks, lettuce, small herbs, spinach, strawberries, young transplants
8–12 inches deep (3–4 gallons)	All herbs, beets (min. 10 inches), bush beans, calendula, carrots (min. 12 inches), chard, marigolds, nasturtiums, radishes (min. 10 inches), shallots
12–15 inches deep (5–8 gallons)	Broccoli, cabbage, cauliflower, celery, collards, corn, cucumbers, eggplants, garlic, kale, melons, onions, peas, peppers, pole beans, potatoes, squash, tomatoes
15–18 inches deep (9–25 gallons)	Mixed plantings, young trees and shrubs
18–24 inches deep (25+ gallons)	Mature trees and shrubs, mixed plantings

I used to believe in lining the bottoms of pots with quick-to-drain materials, like pebbles or stones. But I've found the rocks often block drainage holes and prevent water from spilling out. Lining the base of a pot also artificially moves the level of saturated potting mix higher up in the pot while shrinking the amount of space that roots have to stretch out and grow. Both these factors make root rot more likely, and can stunt plant growth.

What are the signs my plants need a bigger home?

Repotting can be stressful to plants, so do it only if you must. In general, annuals won't need to be repotted if they're seeded or transplanted into a container big enough for them to grow into. But for perennials, sizing up is an important part of keeping them healthy.

If you see one or more of the following signs, it may be time to repot your plants:

- Roots are starting to grow out of the drainage holes.
- Roots are pushing the plant up and out of the container.
- Plant growth has slowed.
- Plants are top-heavy and prone to falling over.
- Potting mix dries out more quickly than usual.

To remove your precious plants from their existing containers, tap or squeeze the sides of each pot before sliding out the plants. If your well-rooted plants are putting up a fight or your container doesn't flex, run a knife around the edge to break the tension.

Once your plant is free, gently massage the bottom of the root ball to release the roots, and break their circular growth pattern, before placing it in its new home. Ease the shock by watering it. Another way to relieve stress is to add a teaspoon of kelp meal per planting hole.

Is it possible to winterize my containers so they don't crack?

Cold weather can do a number on containers. Any water left in potting mix can expand in freezing weather and break them, especially if they're made of porous material. If you don't have the luxury of using a garage or shed to store your fragile pots, protect them against the cold by taking the following steps.

First, clear out any plant debris and scoop out half the potting mix to give it room to expand. To prevent more water from coming in, cover your large pots with plastic tarp and tie it on with a bungee cord. For smaller pots, gather them under a tarp and secure it with something heavy, like a rock. I use neutral-colored tarps rather than the traditional bright blue ones, so they're less of an eyesore.

If you're keeping perennials outdoors year-round, insulate them with thick blankets, burlap, or stacked hay bales. Or simply choose a more durable material, like thick plastic, which can better handle freeze and thaw cycles. (See "Upkeep: Fall," page 137.)

PLANTING

Every July, I harvest several clumps of garlic from a wide barrel on my porch and lay them on the wooden floor to dry. Once the skins are crispy and the stems shriveled, I carefully braid and hang them in my kitchen pantry for safekeeping. The braids, protected from the sun, last all winter long. If I need a head of garlic, I reach into my pantry and snap one off. I can't get enough of it—homegrown garlic is much more flavorful than the bulbs you buy in the store.

So before I run out, usually sometime in February or March, I plant the sprouted ones in fresh potting mix, about two inches deep. Indoor garlic is never as large as bulbs grown with the benefits of the

Drawer with onions: In one of my crazier planter experiments, I picked up a set of drawers from the side of the road and planted onions and peppers in it. It was more of a *why not* than a plan. I drilled a few holes in the bottom and enjoyed it while it lasted. After about two years, the bottom rotted out.

outdoors. Still, if you know a few tricks, like using living soil and adding extra light as needed, it's close enough.

PREPPING YOUR POTS

No matter where you grow it, every container garden starts with preparing your pots and soil mix. If you're planting containers for the first time, and starting with new pots and fresh mix, readying them is pretty straightforward. But if you're working with last year's pots, which likely contain the dried remnants of previous plants, you have a choice.

A number of gardening experts recommend starting plants in clean, or sterilized, pots and new potting soil because it can harbor fungal and bacterial pathogens from the previous season. Signs of disease include sudden death, stunted growth, planted seeds that never sprout, mold growth on leaves like powdery mildew, and dry, curled, or wilted leaves. If your old plants didn't exhibit any of these problems, you can rehab your potting mix rather than toss it, which is what I tend to do.

Every spring, I empty my pots onto a tarp and work on clearing out the old roots, though I don't worry about getting them all, since they can become food for soil organisms. Sifting through the mix, I look for pests like white, squishy grubs or light orange wireworms that eat plant roots, and toss those to the birds.

To replenish the soil's nutrients and life, I add fresh compost or compost-rich potting soil, aiming for a one-to-one mix. In my larger, twenty-gallon-plus-sized pots and beds, I'm nourishing an existing population of healthy soil organisms. With my smaller containers, it's less clear; the fresh compost may just replace what was lost. But the outcome either way is living soil, which is key to promoting a productive garden.

Large planters are different in another way, too: It's impractical to dump out all that potting soil each season, though solarizing is also an option. Unless there's a chance of passing on disease, I leave the potting soil in place and aerate it, jabbing the surface with a trowel or pitchfork to open up pockets of air. Then I scoop out enough of the potting soil to make room for at least four inches of fresh compost. Mix it in, and it's ready to receive fresh seeds and starts.

PLANTING SEEDS, STARTS, OR CUTTINGS

I experiment with different ways to grow plants, but my preference is working with seeds. Starter plants have an obvious benefit—they gift you with an instant garden. But with seeds, you have hundreds more varieties to choose among, like the micro tomato, which grows only eight inches tall and yet somehow produces many handfuls of small, juicy fruit, or the dime-sized Alpine strawberry I eat right off the vine. I often combine starts with seeds to get the benefit of both. There's really no best way to start your garden.

Starting from seeds. Young seedlings are vulnerable to the cold, and pests love the tender shoots. So wait to seed into outdoor containers until after the last winter frost. To give them a sturdier start, you can also grow seeds indoors in early spring in small pots, and transplant them into bigger pots when the weather warms. If you're keeping your tiny victory garden indoors, start your seeds any time.

Read the packet instructions for guidance on planting depth, but don't get bogged down in the details. Seed packets offer spacing guidelines for garden beds, not containers, so you'll have to adapt. For smaller pots, less than two gallons in size, the guidelines may suggest you have room for only one pepper plant or a handful of beets. Since you obviously want to plant more than a few scant seeds—I mean, what if they don't sprout?—I recommend marking where you want your plants, poking holes in the soil, and dropping in at least three seeds per hole.

If you're adding more than one type of plant, say a grouping of basil, tomatoes, and spinach, try to factor in how much space each

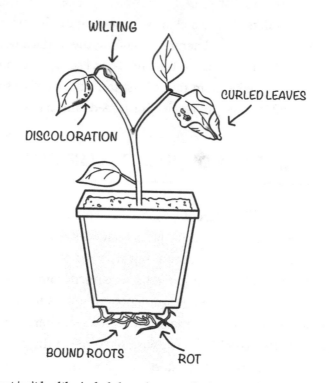

WILTING

CURLED LEAVES

DISCOLORATION

BOUND ROOTS

ROT

Signs your plant isn't healthy include bound roots, wilted or discolored leaves, curled leaves, and brown or black roots.

crop will take up once it fills out. Again, you can't afford to be too precise in pots. Thin your seedlings once they sprout, keeping only the strongest ones. In general, your annuals will sprout first, with perennials emerging later.

Once planted, seeds need a constant, light watering, whether they're inside or outside, to keep the soil surface damp enough to let them sprout. Watering the potting soil with a spray bottle is a good way to apply even moisture.

If you're new to this, allow me to be the first to tell you that spritzing seeds can become a tiresome chore. I beat the need to water daily by placing a dampened piece of burlap or old towel on the soil surface. The wet fabric both adds moisture and helps hold it in. When the fabric dries, soak it in water and reapply. Once your seeds sprout, ditch the burlap so your tender seedlings have room to grow. Another option is to cover your planter with cling wrap to prevent water from evaporating. The clear plastic also makes it easier to see when your seeds pop through the soil, at which point you can remove it.

Planting starts. I may love seeds, but working with baby plants is just simpler. Using them removes the complicated calculus of figuring out how many seeds is enough, they don't need daily watering, and you won't have as long to wait before they fruit.

Most starts need to be relocated since they arrive in small pots. Loosen the soil by squeezing the sides of the pot, or rolling it from side to side. Never yank on the stem to get it out. Once you've removed the plant, separate the roots to encourage a deep dive into the soil, then lower it into its new, bigger pot. If you buy a mature, root-bound perennial, you may need more than your fingers to loosen the roots. I sometimes use a knife to saw off a thin layer from the bottom of the root ball to release them.

Plants are sensitive, just like every living thing, and can get stressed out by change. So after relocating your plants, give them a good drink to minimize the shock, and maybe a spoonful of kelp. If all goes well, your starters will quickly put on new growth—that is, if they start off healthy.

Not every gardening center does a good job of taking care of its plants. Here's what to look for in choosing a healthy one.

Strong roots: Gently tip the plant upside down and out of its pot to check the roots. A plant with brown, dried out, or slimy roots won't grow well. Rotten roots can also smell sulfurous, like bad eggs. Healthy roots are generally white and hold soil firmly in place.

If you see a mat of roots busting out of the bottom of the pot, it's a sign the plant is root-bound and craving a roomier home. (See "What are the signs my plants need a bigger home?" page 68.) This problem is easy to fix for herbaceous plants, which don't have woody stems and include all annuals and a few perennials. They're usually pretty forgiving. Just tease out the mat with your fingers before placing your plant in a new pot or raised bed.

Root-bound woody plants, like fruit trees, are harder to save. If a tree seedling has been neglected for too long, its long root will circle around the bottom of the pot before eventually choking itself.

Fresh-looking foliage: This may seem obvious, but I'm saying it anyway: Buy plants with vibrant green leaves. Yellow, brown, crispy, wilted, curled, or stunted leaves are all signs of insufficient care or a more serious disease issue. Plants that have not received enough light or nutrients will appear stretched out, and thin, and are prone to breakage, pests, and disease. So choose well-branched, bushy plants.

Plant perennial cuttings. I regularly take cuttings of perennial plants I'd like to grow at home, like the delicious chocolate mint I clipped

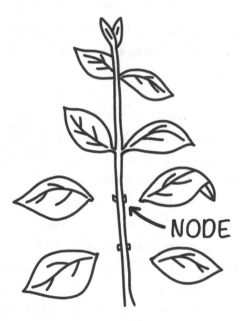

For a stem cutting, snip a bit of stem, at least five inches long, from healthy, unflowered plants in the springtime. Make sure your cutting has at least a few nodes, or tiny notches, where new roots can push out. On the bottom half of your cutting, strip leaves from the nodes.

recently from a friend's yard. Cuttings have the advantage of being free and fairly low-risk, since most work out pretty well. They especially make sense with certain perennials, like berry bushes and some herbs, that take a long time to grow to maturity from seed.

You can propagate nearly all woody perennials from a stem cutting, and even tender perennials, like tomatoes and peppers. I grow many of my berry bushes and fruit trees this way. I use root cuttings for herbs, which can easily regrow from a divided root crown or snippet of root.

Stem cuttings. Snip at least three to five inches from a stem or branch, preferably from new and flexible spring growth. A good cutting should have at least one node, a bump along the stem where a bud attaches, and a few leaves. Place your cutting in a pot at least four inches deep, cut side down, with the leaves above the soil line. If you'd like to speed up the rooting process, dip the cut ends into a

For a root cutting, dig out around the base of a plant and look for a root spreading outwards that's at least as thick as a pen. Snip off a few three-inch pieces.

rooting hormone, like willow extract, before planting. Depending on the plant, it can take anywhere from a few weeks to a couple of months for your cuttings to take root and grow.

Root cuttings. The best time to take root cuttings is in the late fall when plant growth slows. But you can get away with clipping roots any time of the year. Place each cutting in a gallon pot, at least an inch deep. If you're successful, and depending on the type of perennial, new shoots will appear in a few weeks to a few months. Wait until your cutting has at least three leaves before transplanting it into its permanent home.

Upcycle kitchen scraps. The way I grow my garlic is a good example of kitchen-scrap gardening. Basically, it's taking leftover bits you'd otherwise toss in the compost bin, and growing from them. Good candidates include most herbs, the butt ends of leafy vegetables that grow heads, like celery and lettuce, and the root ends of bulbous crops,

A POTTED PLANT'S WATERING NEEDS

How often your potted plants need a drink depends on several factors, including climate, the material of the container, and whether it's living indoors or outdoors.

Weather	High temperatures and full sun, especially in the middle of summer, will dry out your plants surprisingly fast. If you water in the morning, your plants might need another drink by 2 p.m. Wind can dry out plants just as quickly as the sun.
Container type	Terra cotta and fabric pots, though more breathable, will lose moisture more rapidly than plants growing in nonporous containers. Plastic pots, especially dark-colored ones, can bake in the sun and dry out your potting soil.
Container size	Big pots, with their larger soil volume, don't dry out as quickly as small pots, which means your small annuals will need more watering than your larger dwarf trees.
Plant maturity	Established plants, with well-developed root systems, will soak up water more quickly and need frequent drinks.
Indoors or outdoors	Water evaporates more quickly from potting soil when exposed to the wind and sun. So outdoor plants need more water than indoor ones.

like green onions, garlic, chives, leeks and fennel. Place your bit in a shallow saucer of water, refresh it weekly, and it will push out roots and new leafy greens. You can grow most kitchen scraps in water in a sunny spot year-round, or pot them up once they have roots and new leaves. I recommend starting with a few easy herbs, like basil, chives, and mint. Clip a sprig, set it in water, and watch it grow.

Questions

How often do I need to water my plants?

Many people are guilty of loving their plants to death by overwatering them. Your job as a plant caretaker is to keep the soil *evenly moist*. That means soil that is damp, not soggy; it should clump when you squeeze a handful, without dripping any water.

The difference between damp and soggy soil may seem trivial, but it's important for healthy roots, which need air and water to grow. When soil is drenched, the air bubbles trapped between pockets of tiny soil particles fill with water, and the roots can drown. The same goes for soil organisms. One way to prevent overwatering is to place a pile of ice cubes on the potting soil's surface, so it absorbs water slowly as they melt.

Keeping soil damp is a general place to start, but different plants have different watering needs. Herbs like rosemary and thyme prefer to dry out between waterings. Delicate greens, like lettuce, and fleshy fruits, like cucumbers, are very thirsty and require frequent drenchings to produce a good crop. Keep plant tags or seed packages as a reminder of a plant's specific care requirements.

Is there an easy way to keep up with watering demands?

You didn't get into container gardening only to feel shackled to your plants. Any of the following watering hacks will buy you more time between waterings, and even allow you to get out of town now and then.

Bury pots in your pot. In my larger containers, I like to bury a smaller terra cotta pot, leaving only a small lip above the surface. On hot days, I fill the small pot with water and let it slowly drain into the larger container. Since the clay pot absorbs excess water, it also releases moisture as it dries.

Bury a sponge. In one of my favorite hacks, I take a kitchen sponge, cut it into squares, and place the pieces at the bottom of my pots. The sponges soak up excess water, which roots can tap into when the soil dries. The beauty of this approach is that it also helps prevent rot by pulling excess moisture away from your roots.

Insert watering stakes. If your containers don't have the extra space for burying small pots, use watering stakes, which slowly release water through small openings. They're available in many forms, from artistic blown glass orbs to a frugal upside-down water bottle with a small hole in its cap.

Consider drip irrigation. This method sends a slow, steady supply of water through a network of plastic tubing and into each of your pots. You'll need a pressure regulator to manage the water flow rate, which is included in most irrigation kits. I recommend attaching an automatic timer to your water connection so you don't have to worry about turning it off, or on. A drip system can be a little tricky to set up, but you'll be glad you did once you realize how much time it saves.

Try self-watering planters. These are the latest craze in container gardening, for good reason. At the bottom of each of these containers, which are made from heavy-duty plastic, is a reservoir you can fill up with a hose. Most have an overflow hole so any excess water drains away. The soil soaks up the water from the bottom and stays damp, but never soaked. Top off the reservoir once a week and you'll have nicely watered plants.

Do I mulch my newly potted plants?

I am just as much a mulch fanatic as I am a compost zealot. Adding a nice layer of mulch cuts back on the need to water, buffers plants against weather extremes, and helps block unwanted weeds. Organic mulch is also another food source for worms, fungi, and beneficial bacteria.

Layer on at least an inch of whatever mulch you choose after planting your starts or cuttings—fresh seeds need to sprout first. I favor organic mulch, like untreated grass clippings, seaweed, shredded leaves, shredded paper or cardboard, woodchips, and straw. But traditional garden mulch can be a bit messy for indoor plants. Decorative mulch, including pebbles, marbles, Spanish moss, or sea glass, works just fine—use just enough to cover the soil surface.

Decorative mulch, like glass stones, may be more suitable for indoor plants than shredded leaves and straw.

Soil dries out more slowly indoors, since it's sheltered from drying winds and intense sun, and excess mulch invites mold. Before watering, I peek under the mulch to make sure the potting soil is dry.

You won't need to mulch your indoor plants again, unless you're using organic mulch, which will need replenishing if it breaks down. For outdoor plants, mulch again in the fall, when you're tucking in cold-weather perennials and cool-season annuals for the winter. And again in the spring, when you want to conserve moisture, prevent weed growth, and protect your plants from baking in the sun.

CROP PROFILES

My earliest forays into container gardening were fairly timid. I stuck with herbs, for the most part, and the occasional tomato plant. But I've learned since that just about any food crop that does well in a backyard garden will do fine in containers—eggplants, lettuce, and turnips among them. Still, some do better than others; namely, the small ones.

Look for compact fruits and vegetables, and you will find them. Many of my favorite seed companies have piloted breeding programs to meet the demand for small, productive crops that taste good, like the Eros mini bell pepper from Johnny's Selected Seeds, or the container growing collection curated by High Mowing Organic Seeds. The Dwarf Tomato Project, established in 2005, is working with growers

Woven basket: I love the way the nasturtiums and oregano look spilling over the edges of this woven basket, with rosemary standing tall in the center. I added a plastic liner to make sure it's around for a while.

from around the world to find new varieties of small tomatoes, and has thus far come up with seventy.

In the plant profiles that follow, I've listed a few of the compact varieties I particularly like. In addition to the vegetables and herbs, you'll find fruit trees, partly because they're available in dwarf, bush, and miniature varieties. But I also like the way they smell and how long-lasting they are. I've been moving the same lime tree in and out of my dining room for the past four years.

As with most perennials, the trees, blueberry bushes, and other fruits and herbs I've listed settle in for the long haul and grow slowly, which means you don't have to swap them in and out of pots very often. Having some greenery indoors during the drab winter months certainly cheers things up. But I generally favor growing perennials outdoors in the ground because it gives me a chance to further enrich the soil and its carbon-capturing potential. Plus, choosing annuals allows me to maximize crop production in my containers.

To give you plenty of options, I've included a sampling of cold- and warm-season annuals. A few are fast-growing, like salad greens, and others take a while to mature, like beans. For perennials, I've noted in which areas of the country they're likely to thrive by indicating their hardiness zones. (See "The hardiness zone map," page 31.)

To make it easier to put together your garden, I've provided cheat sheets that highlight which plants grow better on windowsills, in outdoor containers, and indoors, and included a few plants in addition to the ones profiled. I've also suggested how to protect against pests (see "Indoor and outdoor organic pest solutions," page 138), and when to use fertilizer (see "Organic soil boosters," page 15).

If you're new to gardening in containers, I recommend starting small with easy-to-grow plants like herbs, especially ones that tolerate hot, dry conditions, such as thyme, oregano, rosemary, and sage. They're forgiving if you forget to water them for a week, or two. If you're not big on herbs, or don't have much sun, go for leafy greens, like spinach and lettuce, which grow quickly and don't need a lot of tending.

After mastering these easier-to-grow varieties, consider moving on to something more advanced, like planting a combination of tomatoes, basil, and hot peppers in the same container. You can't really go wrong if you choose fruits and vegetables you like to eat, and pay attention to what they need.

Finally, it's possible you'll be seeing a twisted carrot or sun-spotted pepper for the first time. The sight can be jarring if you're accustomed to gleaming, pockmark-free supermarket produce. But I'm guessing your reaction may be more along the lines of, *Well, damn, I just grew a pepper!* For most of us, growing our own crisp spicy peppers or jewel-toned beets from seeds or starts never gets old.

CROP CHEAT SHEETS

Use these cheat sheets to figure out what you want to grow given your space and experience. I recommend starting with easy herbs, shade-tolerant leafy greens, and root crops that you can grow inside on a windowsill. Dedicate the corner of your living room to annuals and perennials that can live indoors with some extra light and space. Then, if you want bigger plantings and have some sunny real estate, consider plants that like to live outdoors for at least part of the year. Construct mixed planters with thrillers, fillers, and spillers (I've included my favorites in this chart). Find out what plants you can grow from food scraps. And get to know a few pollinator magnets so you can cultivate a diverse, wildlife-friendly garden.

Easy annuals you can grow on a windowsill	Arugula, basil, celery, chard, cilantro, collards, kale, lettuce, parsley, spinach
Annuals you can grow indoors with extra light	Beets, broccoli, bush beans, cabbage, carrots, cauliflower, onions, potatoes, radishes
Annuals that grow better outdoors	Corn, cucumbers, eggplants, marigolds, melons, nasturtiums, peas, pole beans, squash
Perennials you can grow indoors year-round	Basil, chives, garlic, leaf fennel, mint, oregano, peppers, radicchio, rosemary, sage, scallions, sorrel, thyme, tomatoes
Perennials you can grow outdoors year-round	Blackberries, blueberries, chives, currants, garlic, goji berries, grapes, hardy fruit trees, huckleberries, mint, oregano, raspberries, rhubarb, runner beans, sage, scallions, sorrel, strawberries, thyme
Perennials you need to bring inside for the winter	Artichokes, avocados, basil, citrus, oregano, peppers, rosemary, sub-tropical and tropical fruit trees, tomatoes
Plants you can regrow from kitchen scraps	Basil, cabbage, celery, chives, cilantro, garlic, leeks, lettuce, mint, onions, potatoes, scallions
Pollinator magnets	Asters, bee balm, borage, calendula, coneflowers, heliotrope, lavender, lemon balm, marigolds, nasturtiums, purple tansy, salvia, sweet alyssum, thyme, yarrow, zinnias
Thrillers	Peas, peppers, pole beans, tomatoes, trellised vines
Fillers	Carrots, chard, chives, lettuce, marigolds, radishes, spinach
Spillers	Cucumbers, melons, nasturtiums, oregano, squash, strawberries, thyme

HERBS

Basil

Annual and perennial
Crop type: warm
Perennial varieties hardiness zone: 10

We all know and love the sweet basil commonly used in pesto, but it's an annual and lasts only one season. Perennial basil is a container-garden hero because the tender young leaves can be harvested year-round when the plant is sheltered from the cold. Hailing from the tropical regions of Asia and Africa, it possesses a more complex, spicy flavor. If you want to give perennial basil a chance look for tulsi, hoary, or wild basil. There's some old garden lore that praises basil's ability to make other crops taste better. I believe it—especially when it's near my tomatoes. Placing your basil pots around the edges of outdoor seating areas can also help keep away mosquitos.

Planting

Basil loves warm temperatures and southern exposure where it can soak up as much sunlight as possible. It grows robust roots, so give it a deep container. Sweet basil grows up to a foot and a half tall, with green to purple foliage and white or purple flowers. Perennial basil grows to double that size and has a more shrub-like habit. To provide some support, especially for plants in windier areas, I like to create an X out of bamboo poles or stakes and drive it into the potting soil to prop up the plant and take some weight off the stem.

Indoors. In cooler climates, move your annuals and perennials indoors into a well-lit room when chilly weather arrives. Your sweet basil will last a few more months. But perennial basil can continue to flower and produce tasty leaves all winter under grow lights. In the spring, after the first frost has passed, move your perennial basil back outside.

Kitchen scrap contender: Propagating new basil plants, either annual or perennial, is a cinch. Snip some cuttings off your old basil plant and place them in a glass of water. In a few weeks, each cutting should be growing roots. When the roots are at least an inch long, plant your baby sprigs together in a four-inch-deep pot.

Upkeep

If you're growing sweet basil, the best way to preserve its strong flavor is to pinch off the flower buds before they bloom. Once the plant produces seed, the leaves can turn bitter tasting and stop growing. Pinching will become a regular chore, since plants try to re-bloom over and over until the late-season chill takes hold. For your perennial basil, on the other hand, give it permission to bloom since it won't really change the taste. Trim your plants in the spring and fall to contain any runaway growth, and produce a lovely summer bloom that attracts pollinators.

Challenges

Pests. Basil suffers from grazing by aphids, slugs, Japanese beetles, and flea beetles. One summer I had a frustrating flea beetle problem that swarmed my plants, peppering them with tiny pinhole bites that left the leaves discolored and stressed. While most pests are easily controlled with an insecticidal soap or neem oil spray, flea beetles are relentless and the only defense is to cover your plants with lightweight fabric, or lure them away with a trap crop, like arugula or radish.

Disease. Basil planted in well-drained soil grows well without the threat of disease. In muggy and humid climates, fungal diseases like mildew or black spot can be a concern. Even so, they won't develop until well into the growing season, so you can get in a good harvest

Perennial basil, which grows twice the size of sweet basil, branches out like a shrub with flowers that supply pollinators with sweet nectar.

before any damage occurs. If your plants show signs of disease, switch out the soil in your container before planting more; the fungal spores can overwinter in the soil, and resurface the following spring.

Harvest

Harvest up to two-thirds of your basil plant at a time, or pick leaves and stems as needed. I tend to pinch off the first three leaves from the top, which have the most flavor. Regular clipping encourages new growth. Basil is best used fresh, pretty much as soon as it's picked. In refrigerators, it goes brown. For short-term use, stick a stem on your kitchen counter in a glass of room-temperature water to keep clipped sprigs fresh for longer.

Chives

Perennial
Hardiness zone: 3

Chives are beautiful plants that can grow year-round both indoors and outdoors. Outdoors, this hardy perennial goes dormant in the winter season, only to flush up new growth in the spring. Pollinators love their pom-pom-shaped purple or white flowers. Garden chives are the most common species grown in North America and have a subtle onion flavor. But I prefer growing the garlic chive, a smaller plant that blooms white, star-shaped flowers and carries a hint of garlic flavor. Chives are among the first plants to sprout in early spring, but can also grow in hot, dry climates as long as you keep them well-watered. Unlike most herbs, they prefer rich, moist soil loaded with organic matter.

Planting

Chives typically reach eighteen inches high and can be divided into smaller pots if they get too big. I scatter them throughout my vegetable containers to add a pop of color and as a natural pest deterrent.

Kitchen scrap contender: You can regrow chives indoors from the base of an old chive plant. After you've finished cooking with the chives, keep two to three inches of the plant attached to the bulbs and plant them in a pot with soil mix. Add only enough soil to cover the roots to keep the stems high and dry.

Indoors. Chive plants in large containers can last outdoors through the winter, but I recommend moving any plants growing in small containers indoors because potted perennials are less hardy than those grown in the ground. Chives need just four to six hours of sunlight a day and can handle the low-light conditions of winter.

Upkeep

Chives grow in big clumps that can outgrow a pot over the course of a few seasons. In the cool temperatures of the spring or fall, take your chives out of the pot and divide the bulbs into four equal sections. Repot each section into its own container or pass some on to a friend. If the leaves of your indoor chives become tired and withered in the winter, your plant may need a rest. Cut back its foliage to two inches above the soil level and place your pot in the fridge for two to three weeks. Then return your plant to room temperature, give it some water, and watch for new growth.

Challenges

Pests. Chives act as an excellent pest repellent for cabbage worms, aphids, and carrot flies, making them a particularly good companion for cilantro, tomatoes, carrots, and cabbage. Occasionally onion thrips can pester your plants, but it's easy to remove them with a good blast of water from a hose.

Disease. Chives are related to other alliums like onions and garlic, and can suffer from the same fungal disease, which is called allium rust. Lower the risk by watering the soil around your plants, keeping the leaves dry.

Harvest

Like most herbs, the plant's flavor peaks just before it blooms in May or June; the flowers are just as tasty as the leaves. If you have a new chive plant, wait to harvest it until the plant grows at least six inches and has multiple leaves. After that, you can harvest the herb at any time of the year. Snip the hollow leaves at the base of the plant. Chives store well at room temperature if you place the leaves cut side down in a cup of water for up to a week.

Cilantro or Coriander

Annual
Crop type: cool

Freshly harvested cilantro is an excellent source of potassium and is said to aid digestion. It also attracts aphid-devouring beneficials, like lacewings and ladybugs, while being somewhat immune to aphid damage itself. This makes the herb a perfect bug trap. Aphids and the insects that eat them will flock to cilantro, and stay off any neighboring plants. Some varieties promote superb leafy growth, and others produce more seeds, known as coriander. Slow-to-bolt varieties like Long Standing or Calypso can extend your harvest in warmer months. If it's the earthy-tasting seeds you're after, choose a variety like Santo.

Planting

Cilantro can grow just about anywhere. It prefers sunny, cool springs and can even handle a light frost. In warmer climates, cilantro will benefit from afternoon shade. It has a deep tap root that needs lots of room, so grow it in a pot at least ten inches deep. If you give it enough space, your cilantro will be more resilient in hot and dry conditions, and you won't have to water it as often.

Indoors. Because cilantro is a short-lived annual, it's not worth trying to extend the harvest by moving it indoors for the winter. For a continuous harvest, start new plants again from seed or buy transplants. You can grow cilantro entirely indoors if you give your plants at least six hours of bright light a day from a south-facing window or grow lights.

Kitchen scrap contender: Like basil, cilantro stems easily root in a glass of water. For best results, change out the water every few days. When roots have grown a couple inches long, plant the stems in a fresh pot of soil and watch for new growth.

Upkeep

This herb grows quickly in the cooler spring and fall months but comes to a near halt once temperatures rise and it puts its energy into growing flowers and seed, rather than leaves.

Challenges

Pests. White flies and aphids love to visit cilantro plants, especially once the plants are stressed from the summer heat. In some cases you'll want to spray plants with an insecticidal soap or neem oil to protect them.

Disease. This herb can succumb to powdery mildew. Avoid watering its leaves to prevent an outbreak that can spread to other plants.

Harvest

To harvest the leafy greens, snip them from the base of the plant when they're about six inches high. You can pick up to a third of the plant at a time without stressing it out. If it's the coriander seeds you're after, clip the seed heads into a paper bag, seal it, and shake the seeds free. The seeds will be ready to use in the kitchen. Cilantro can self-sow into surrounding pots if you're not careful; just yank the baby plants if you'd rather it didn't.

Mint

Perennial
Hardiness zone: 3

Mint is a mighty, fast-growing plant that's a pollinator magnet when in bloom. My personal favorites, chocolate and Moroccan mint, have a heavenly smell that keeps mosquitoes at bay during summer nights out on my porch. Mint is a perennial in even the coldest climates in the United States. However, once the winter chill sets in it goes dormant and the foliage dies back. You can leave it outside, or bring it inside before a frost to keep it growing all year. Your mint may still die back in the fall, but as long as you keep the soil moist it will return to life later on—just in time for fresh mint tea or even a boozy mint julep in the middle of winter.

Planting

Mint grows well with almost anything as long as you don't let it take over. It spreads so quickly you'll only need to grow one plant per eight-inch-wide container. Encourage its sprawling growth to cascade over the sides of your container for a lush look.

Indoors. Though most herbs prefer a well-lit, south-facing window, mint is a plant that appreciates some partial shade. The indirect light of an east- or west-facing window will usually do. Don't let your mint dry out, since it likes moist soil. Keep the air around it humid by placing it near other plants or spritzing it weekly with water. Pinch off flowers as buds develop to encourage foliage growth.

Kitchen scrap contender: It's easy to create new mint plants on your kitchen counter. Trim five-to-six-inch pieces from your mature plants and remove the leaves from the bottom third of the cutting. Then place the bottom end into a glass of water and watch the magic happen. Once the roots have grown a couple inches long, stick your cutting into a fresh pot of potting soil.

Upkeep

Mint is an excellent container herb in part because it can be a brute when planted in the ground. This quick-spreading herb tends to conquer a space. Pull out large portions of the plant periodically to make sure it doesn't crowd itself out of its pot—or just keep moving it into bigger containers. If your mint looks gangly you can encourage a bushier plant by pruning it into a ball shape and letting it grow back out.

Challenges

Pests. Mint's sprawling underground root systems can fall prey to soil pests like root borers, cutworms, and root weevils. Unless you have a dire infestation, your mint plants can handle the underground attack. Sprinkle diatomaceous earth (DE) and gently mix it into the first few inches of soil to deter soft-bodied soil pests.

Disease. Not much bothers this tough little plant. It can occasionally get fungal rots like wilt or rust if it's overwatered or planted in a location with poor airflow. Space out the plants to encourage good circulation.

Harvest

Mint is a breeze to harvest and its fast growth means there will always be something to clip. You can harvest individual leaves or hasten its growth by snipping a few sprigs from the base of the plant. Mint is most flavorful before it flowers, but you can harvest its leaves any time.

Oregano

Perennial
Hardiness zone: 4

Oregano is a hardy, heat-loving, and drought-tolerant herb that isn't picky about soil. The fact that it can grow vigorously without much tending makes it a gratifying starter plant. There are two distinct types of oregano: Mexican and Mediterranean. Both types thrive in pots, and both taste similar, though it's possible to pick up subtle notes of citrus in Mexican oregano. This fragrant herb is a friend to all plants, and some gardeners claim it can improve the health of its neighbors. I've never tested this, but I like the idea.

Planting

Oregano can grow as an annual almost anywhere in the United States, and as a perennial in places that stay above 10 degrees in the winter. Its flavor is strongest when planted in full sun. Because it's highly adaptable to dry conditions, you won't have to spend much time on watering. Oregano is in the mint family, and just like mint is a vigorous grower. Keep one plant per six-inch-wide pot so it has plenty of room to stretch its roots.

Indoors. Move this plant indoors for the winter before your first fall frost, and back outdoors once nightly temperatures have reached 55 degrees. You can also grow oregano on a windowsill year-round. The brighter the room the better, since oregano likes six to eight hours of full sun a day. If you live in a northern climate, consider setting up a grow light during the winter for optimal growth.

Upkeep

Keep your oregano full and healthy by snipping off the new tips of stems to encourage bushier growth and control its overall height. Oregano is pretty prolific, so pinch off the flowers before they go to seed to prevent unwelcome plants. When my plants get too big, I divide them in the fall and put the extra plants in indoor pots.

Challenges

Pests. Oregano occasionally attracts spider mites and aphids. Though this sturdy plant won't be bothered by them, nearby fruits and vegetables will be, so treat pests with an organic pesticide like neem oil or insecticidal soap.

Disease. Oregano is nearly bulletproof when it comes to disease. As with all plants in the mint family, giving this herb a little space will improve air circulation and help prevent fungal mint rust.

Harvest

Start picking your oregano once stems are about eight inches tall. The more you pick, the more it will grow. As with most herbs, the flavor peaks before it flowers in the mid-to-late summer.

Rosemary

Perennial
Hardiness zone: 7

Native to the Mediterranean region, rosemary is drought-tolerant and best grown in hot and dry climates. In cold regions, where temperatures frequently drop below 20 degrees, it grows as an annual

Rosemary likes its soil dry and absorbs moisture through its leaves. Keep your plant happy indoors by misting the foliage a couple of times a week.

unless you bring it inside for the winter. The herb comes in a whole suite of shapes and sizes, from large shrubs to low-creeping groundcovers. Certain varieties, like Tuscan Blue or Blue Spires, fare better for cooking than others because of their high oil content. If you live in a cool and damp climate, grow cold-hardy varieties like Arp or Hill Hardy, which tolerate cool and soggy soil. Rosemary's woody camphor smell makes it an excellent pest deterrent.

Planting

Upright rosemary varieties can grow quite large, so plant them in a pot at least ten inches wide and deep for the best results. Creeping rosemary can survive in smaller pots six to eight inches in diameter. To prevent the roots from sitting in soggy soil, plant your rosemary in containers made from breathable materials like terra cotta or fabric bags.

Indoors. Rosemary won't need much attention when living outside. But inside, give it the brightest, sunniest room available. If you notice your plant thinning after spending some time indoors, add a few supplemental grow lights. Rosemary's growth naturally slows during the winter and it won't need as much watering. It absorbs moisture through its leaves, a natural adaptation to living in dry climates. Since indoor air tends to be drier, try to mist it regularly.

Upkeep

Rosemary takes its time settling before growth kicks in, and then you may want to control it so it doesn't get too big. Trim plants in the spring after they flower, or take cuttings and divide your plants in the fall, repotting the ones you want to keep. If you leave your container outside, mulch it to insulate the roots against the cold. The plant will go dormant and stop growing in winter, though its leaves will remain evergreen. During particularly harsh cold snaps, even cold-hardy varieties will appreciate the chance to shelter in a garage or basement; be sure to water them occasionally. Once spring arrives, push aside the mulch to let the soil warm up more quickly.

Challenges

Pests. Despite this herb's strong smell, pests like mealybugs, spider mites, and whiteflies can be a problem. Regular pruning to increase air circulation helps prevent these pests from becoming an infestation.

Disease. Fungal diseases like mildews and root rots are the most common problem, especially in damp soil or humid areas. Keep your rosemary in loose, well-drained soil and avoid overwatering.

Harvest

Harvest up to two-thirds of the plant at a time. Rosemary is slow to regrow, but regular clipping will help keep your plant healthy and robust.

Thyme

Perennial
Hardiness zone: 5

A relative of oregano, thyme is another great choice for first-time growers since it flourishes with very little attention. It prefers dry, sunny conditions and is forgiving of the forgetful gardener who may not water it regularly. There's a type of thyme for every climate, though not all are fragrant enough for cooking. The best culinary varieties include French, lemon, carraway, orange, and English thyme. I love it because it can survive New England's cold winters; it will go dormant but returns with vigor once spring circles back around.

Planting

Thyme is low growing and can handle a smaller, shallower pot than other herbs. I plant thyme in six-inch-wide, bowl-shaped pots with plenty of drainage holes. It's a natural companion to other low-growing herbs that share the same minimal watering needs, like oregano.

Indoors: Shelter this perennial indoors to enjoy it year-round. Indoor care is very similar to outdoor care. Occasional watering and bright light from a south- or west-facing window are all that it needs.

Upkeep

Thyme loves to spread out, filling in any empty space or gracefully spilling out of your pot. During the first year, avoid clipping your plant in the fall since cutting back new growth will zap it of the energy it needs to survive the winter. A layer of mulch can help your plants handle freezing winter temperatures. Thyme grows so quickly you may need to repot it once a season.

Challenges

Pests. In dry weather, spider mites can plague your plants. Keep infestations in check by spraying them with neem oil or an insecticidal soap.

Disease. Since thyme prefers dry soil, it can develop root rot and other fungal issues in humid conditions. Give your plants plenty of space to increase airflow and help keep them healthy.

Harvest

Harvest thyme whenever you want after the first year.

FRUITS

Avocados

Perennial
Hardiness zone: 8

I've been growing an avocado tree in my dining room for a couple of years now. It's a Little Cado, also known as Wurtz, and happens to be the only true dwarf type, growing just ten to twelve feet high. It also pollinates on its own, unlike most avocado trees. The Little Cado variety opens both female and male flowers at the same time, which means it can self-fertilize. Since other varieties open male and female flowers at different times, you'll need more than one tree to improve the chances of a successful harvest. I'd just go with the Little Cado, which is consistently recommended as the best one for containers.

Planting

As cute as a sprouting avocado pit is on your kitchen windowsill, it won't turn into a fruiting tree. Even if you waited the decade, or more, that it would take to grow, the fruit wouldn't be worth it. Pit-grown avocados don't produce the same quality fruit as their parents. Choose an established young tree from a nursery instead. At a nursery, avocado cuttings are grafted onto healthy, disease-free rootstock.

Plant your tree in a wide container to give roots a chance to spread out. Avocado trees appreciate their own space, so they aren't the best companion-planting candidates. But placing herbs and flowering plants nearby will attract beneficial insects—ones that can boost fruit production and fight off pests.

Indoors. Avocados are well-suited to a controlled indoor environment since they don't like conditions that are too cold or too hot. But I don't recommend growing them entirely indoors; they're more productive if they can bask in the sun for at least part of the year. And while it's possible to keep them alive inside, they'll produce so little fruit the extra effort may not be worth it. So after the last spring frost, when your avocado tree has bloomed, move it outside to be pollinated. Some trees take an entire year to produce full-grown fruit.

Upkeep

Apply fertilizer twice a year to deal with the shock of moving inside in the late fall and back outside in the spring—a quarter cup of potassium-rich kelp meal per five gallons of potting mix will do the trick. Mulch your plant in the spring, and leave a few inches of space around the trunk to prevent rot. Prune leggy branches as you see them to manage for size, and hold off on any heavy pruning until late winter.

Challenges

Pests. While avocados are relatively problem-free, you may find some damage from thrips and mites. If you notice an infestation, spray your tree with a neem oil solution or insecticidal soap.

Disease. Make sure your container is well drained because avocado roots are prone to rot.

Harvest

Flowers pollinated in early spring are ready to harvest from May to September. Avocados don't ripen on the tree. Pick them when they've reached their full size and they'll ripen on your kitchen counter, at room temperature.

Blackberries & Raspberries

Perennial
Hardiness zone: 3

Bramble fruit may conjure up images of thorny, unruly plants best suited for property-line hedgerows. But you can find relatively easy-to-grow thornless and upright varieties that, with proper pruning, will reward you with fruit fit for the gods. Try growing Arapaho, Navaho, or Chester blackberries, which stand four to six feet. Thornless, compact varieties are becoming popular for container growers. Varieties like Raspberry Shortcake® and Mini-Me® are raspberries specifically bred to reach just two to three feet, making them a good pick for patio pots. While it's possible to grow blackberries in any hardiness zone, raspberries prefer climates with cool summers. In milder climates, gardeners can grow at least one heat-tolerant raspberry called Bababerry.

Planting

While brambles have perennial roots and crowns, their canes, or woody stems, are biennial, which means they stop producing fruit after two years. Summer-bearing bramble varieties produce fruit in the summer, but only on canes that are two years old. Fall-bearing varieties produce fruit during their first year of growth. I like to grow a few of each so I have berries during most of the growing season.

You can buy your brambles as bare-rooted canes, or pick up little plants or cuttings to plant outside in early spring. Raise your raspberries and blackberries in half-barrels or in pots at least two feet wide by two feet deep. One half-barrel-sized container will hold about four or five new canes.

Indoors. Don't worry about trying to try to fit these shrubs through your doorway. These cold-hardy perennials can survive the winter with a thick application of mulch in the fall. You can also bring your pots into a sheltered location like an unheated garage or greenhouse, or wrap them in heavy blankets, if you're worried about them cracking in the winter cold.

Upkeep

Brambles constantly replenish themselves with new canes, and will become a tangled mess without regular pruning. Trimming out old canes that no longer produce fruit also makes room for new fruit-bearing canes. For summer-bearing varieties, cut out canes after their second year of growth and leave all first-year growth to fruit the following year. For fall-bearing varieties, simply cut all canes to the base after harvesting the berries and new canes will emerge in the spring. Feed your plants with some compost when you plant them and every year thereafter in early spring.

Challenges

Pests. If you notice wilted tips, your raspberry and blackberry canes have likely been infected by the larvae of tiny boring beetles. To prevent an infestation, prune out the wilted tips. Your biggest pest challenges will likely be birds and squirrels. I've even caught my farm dog, Nimbus, grazing on berries. To avoid sharing your harvest, cover your plants in netting before the fruit ripens.

Disease. Fruit rots and powdery mildews can crop up in warm, humid regions and infect ripe fruit. It'll look like your berries are wearing a

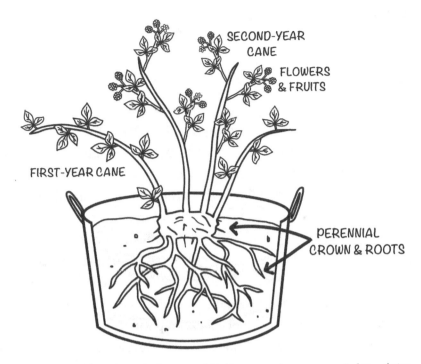

SECOND-YEAR CANE

FLOWERS & FRUITS

FIRST-YEAR CANE

PERENNIAL CROWN & ROOTS

Summer-bearing brambles only flower and fruit on second-year canes. In late winter, prune these old canes back to the base of the plant to make room for more growth.

fuzzy sweater. Prevent these diseases by picking berries before they're overripe. Also, take care not to overwater your plants or wet their foliage or ripening berries. Blackberries are particularly susceptible to cane galls, large bumps that cause canes to swell and split. Prune these out when you notice them. Rust, visible as orange-yellow dots on canes and leaves, can also be a problem. Though it won't affect your berry harvest, rust can dry out leaves and stunt growth, and be passed along to other crops like alliums. Again, prune out any infected canes to stop the spread.

Harvest

Pick your blackberries when they've turned a deep black in July or August. Different raspberries ripen at different times from June to September. Pick them in the cooler hours of the morning when they're firm.

Blueberries

Perennial
Hardiness zone: 3

Blueberries are among my favorite container fruits. Pots make it easier to manage the soil pH for these acid-loving berries. Blueberry bushes also come in container-friendly sizes, like the half-high-bush species, which grows three to four feet high, or the even more diminutive low-bush. Within these compact species, you can choose dwarf varieties like the Northblue half-high or Tophat lowbush. The fruits are small-ish, but they're still sweet. Some blueberry plants need a partner to produce fruit. Even if your blueberry can pollinate itself—and most can—buddy plants that cross-pollinate will give you more and juici-er berries. I have three different types of potted up blueberries that I place no more than five feet apart. Blueberries can take as long as five years to produce a lot of berries.

Planting

Buy blueberries as bare root plants, which are easiest to ship, or as better established rooted cuttings or potted plants. Check the variety for pollinating requirements and whether it might be helpful to have more than one bush. Plant blueberries outside in the late fall or early spring in an acidic potting mix. For a climate-friendly option, choose a blend made with coconut coir and add your own acidifying agents, like organic gypsum (calcium sulfate) or elemental sulfur. You're aim-ing for an optimal pH range of 4.5 to 5.5 and can check it with a simple pH test kit. Blueberries need about four hours of sun a day to produce fruit, but the more time they get to sunbathe, the more fruit they'll give you.

Indoors. There's no need to move your plants indoors for the win-ter, and in fact it's better if you don't. All blueberry plants require a certain number of chill hours, or temperatures below 45 degrees, to produce fruit. You do need to insulate them, however, since container plants are vulnerable to the cold. Shelter them in an unheated shed or garage, and water them occasionally if the soil appears cracked and dry. Or keep them warm outdoors with a heavy layer of straw mulch. For extra protection, I sometimes wrap their containers with burlap or a heavy blanket.

Upkeep

Blueberry plants do just fine in nutrient-poor soil, so don't bother with extra fertilizer unless you notice problems, like the leaves turning reddish-yellow while the veins stay green, which can indicate your berries need a boost in trace minerals, like iron and magnesium. It's more important to maintain acidity. You can keep the pH low by watering the soil occasionally with an apple cider or white vinegar solution (two tablespoons of vinegar per gallon of water) or mulching with oak leaves, pine needles, or an organic soil amendment made from cottonseed meal. Other plants won't enjoy the low pH so grow blueberries in their own pot. Prune your plants in the winter when they're dormant. Cut back on a few of the oldest canes, or primary branches, so the plant can put its energy toward new fruit-producing stems.

Challenges

Pests. Blueberries don't suffer from many pest problems, but birds can decimate your berries in minutes. The solution is easy enough. Cover your plants with netting or chicken wire right before the fruits start turning a purple hue. Keep an eye out for smaller pests, too, like scale, which can look like scabs, and spotted wing drosophila, a destructive fruit fly. Cut out infested branches and spray your plant with neem oil.

Disease. The fungal disease mummy berry attacks blueberry plants by living in fallen, rotting fruit during the winter and sending out spores that kill new growth in the spring. To help prevent this rather serious disease, remove any fallen fruit from around your plant in the fall.

Harvest

Pick blueberries by hand when they're deep blue with a dusty coat. They freeze well for up to a year. (Mine rarely make it to the freezer.)

Citrus

Perennial
Hardiness zone: 8

With their glossy leaves, tropical flowers, and vibrant fruit, citrus trees are a stunning addition to a container garden. Some call them princess plants for the extra attention they need, but caring for them doesn't have to be complicated and a single tree can give you fruit all winter. Any citrus tree grown on a dwarfing rootstock, like Flying Dragon, will grow well in a container. Citrus trees don't appreciate sharing their pots with any other crops, which can disturb their roots and compete for nutrients.

Lemons. Meyer Improved lemon, hardy to 20 degrees, is a hybrid between a lemon and an orange. If you're looking for a more acidic and tart lemon, try growing Eureka.

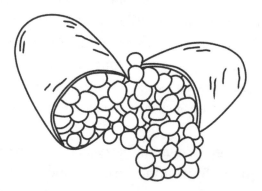

With a little care, and plenty of fertilizer, it's possible to grow exotic tropical delicacies, like Finger limes, indoors.

Limes. Bearss lime is a seedless variety commonly sold at grocery stores. Finger limes produce fruits filled with caviar-like beads of juice inside.

Oranges/Mandarins. The Calamondin orange, hardy down to 20 degrees, is a compact cross between a tangerine and a kumquat. The Satsuma mandarin produces seedless fruit and grows well in mild climates with cool summers.

Kumquats. Naturally compact, Nagami kumquat is cold-hardy to temperatures as low as 18 degrees and the most popular type grown in the United States.

Planting

Plant your trees outside in the spring after the danger of frost has passed, or indoors at any time. If your tree has been grafted onto a rootstock, take care not to add potting soil above the graft union, a noticeable bump on the trunk about five inches above the root ball. Citrus trees don't like having "wet feet" or roots that sit in water, so be careful not to overwater. Clay terra cotta pots, which are somewhat air-permeable, can help prevent your trees from sitting for long in soggy soil.

Indoors. Citrus trees are native to tropical and subtropical regions of the world and cannot survive outside year-round in frost-prone places. If you live in a snowy, cold clime, get used to moving your trees indoors every winter. Moving large planters can be back-breaking, so I recommend investing in a plant trolley. Of course you can also choose to keep your trees indoors all the time.

The most important factor when deciding on an indoor location is—you guessed it—light. Citrus trees need bright sunlight from a south- or southwest-facing window. In higher northern latitudes, consider supplementing your plant's exposure with a grow light. Avoid placing your plants near heaters or vents, which can dry them out. In the winter, your plants will stay evergreen but won't grow as quickly, which means you won't have to water them as often.

Upkeep

Once a year, remove any suckers growing out of the plant's base. These shoots won't produce any fruit and will only use up your tree's precious energy. Don't worry about pruning out interior branches or criss-crossed branches, because thinning your tree's canopy can harm it. If you want to control for size, prune back some of the leggy branches on the outside of the canopy. Time your pruning for late winter or early spring, before new leaves bud out.

Your citrus trees will need regular, deep waterings. Give them a drink when the first inch of soil is dry. Citrus trees are heavy feeders, too—more so than most of my other crops. So every year, I mix plenty of compost or worm castings into the first few inches of potting soil.

Challenges

Pests. Keep an eye out for piercing-sucking pests like aphids, whiteflies, mealybugs, leafminers, and scale. Most of these small insects can be blasted away with water or killed with applications of insecticidal soap. But scale, which have a protective coating, can only be banished with regular applications of horticulture oil. Leaf miners go after new growth in spring and can seriously damage young plants, but don't worry; your citrus trees can handle it and will likely make a full recovery. For indoor plants, spider mites can be a problem. Take your plants outside to hose them off or spray them down with neem oil.

Disease. Black, sooty mold can develop on leaves from the honeydew droppings of sucking insects like aphids and scale. This stuff is problematic since it can interfere with light and photosynthesis. Use soapy water to wash the sooty mold away. Citrus canker and other fungal wood rots are another threat. Prevent their spread by pruning out

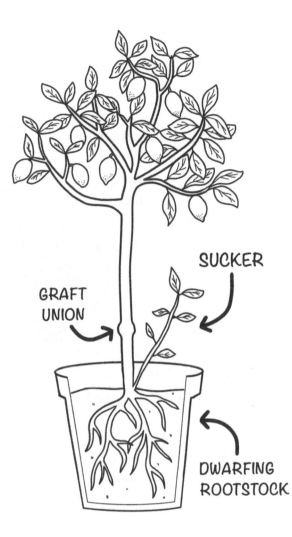

GRAFT
UNION

SUCKER

DWARFING
ROOTSTOCK

Suckers grow from the base of the tree, below the graft union. Prune them out once a year, so your tree can focus on growing more fruit-producing branches in its canopy.

infected branches. It's a good idea to sterilize your pruners between cuts by dipping them in rubbing alcohol.

Harvest

Use pruners or scissors to cut off pieces of fruit, or wait until they drop. One exception is limes. Fully ripe limes are actually yellow, wrinkly, and too bitter to enjoy, so harvest them when they're light green.

Strawberries

Perennial
Hardiness zone: 3

Strawberries are the ultimate container fruit, since they're naturally compact and shallow-rooted. You can choose among dozens of varieties, from June-bearing, the most popular and widely grown strawberry, to day-neutral, which produce berries all the way from spring until your first frost, to Alpine, which produce petite berries. There are strawberries for every region and microclimate, and they all appreciate full sun.

Planting

Strawberries are such popular container plants they have their own special pots, called strawberry urns. They also grow well from hanging baskets, grow bags, planter boxes that attach to the tops of railings, and pyramid planters. Plant your berries as bare-root crowns or established seedlings in early spring.

Indoors. When cool weather hits, strawberries stop growing. Since they're perennials, they need this winter rest period. If your strawberry varieties grow well in your hardiness zone, just leave them outside. But I do recommend mulching them with straw and wrapping their pots with burlap or another heavy fabric for insulation. If you live where the winters are very cold, consider moving them into a sheltered location like a garage, and check on them monthly. If you see dry and cracked soil give them a light watering. As with blueberries, strawberries need a certain number of chill hours in order to fruit.

Upkeep

Strawberries have few maintenance requirements other than regular watering and fertilizing. I mulch my containers every year to help conserve moisture. During the growing season, I give my day neutral varieties a monthly feed of phosphorus-rich fertilizer to keep the everbearing blooms plentiful. Some gardeners like to pinch off all the flowers the first year for a more prolific crop the following year. Since these short-lived perennials need to be replaced every three years anyway, I say skip the extra work and harvest what you can.

Challenges

Pests. Many gardeners prefer growing strawberries in containers because it lifts them off the ground, making them less susceptible to the pests and diseases in the soil. Your biggest nuisance will probably be birds. To prevent feathered berry lovers from getting to your crop before you do, cover your plants with netting. I like to hide my berries underneath leafy vegetables, like lettuce. Occasionally, the tarnished plant bug and bud weevil can zero in on your plants. Pick off any that you see or spray them with insecticidal soap.

Strawberry urns are pots with multiple pockets out of which you can grow shallow-rooted plants, like spinach, lettuce, and, yes, strawberries.

Disease. Strawberry plants can succumb to root rot if they sit in soggy soil, so take care not to overwater. If they get infected, repot your plants with fresh soil in a sterilized container. Your precious berries can also be lost to a gray fluffy mold if they touch dead leaves or the soil, so keep your fruit off the soil.

Harvest

Once berries start ripening, check your pots every day and snatch them up before the birds do. If you see any pale, white splotches on the berries, give them more time to fully ripen. To prevent flavor loss, store any extra berries in bags in your freezer.

VEGETABLES

Beans

Annual and perennial
Crop type: warm
Hardiness zone: 4

Beans are among my favorite vegetables to grow because they throw off lush foliage and come in many varieties. A member of the legume family, beans work with rhizobia bacteria to naturally add nitrogen to the soil. Bush beans, which grow out rather than up, are compact, sturdy, and suitable for pots. The French Mascotte is small and bred specifically for containers, making it a great choice. The fava bean is another option. Pole beans, on the other hand, are tall and require vertical support, but can make spectacular outdoor pot "thrillers."

The best-known pole bean is Blue Lake, the green bean we're all familiar with in supermarkets. Other examples include the kidney bean and the scarlet runner bean, a perennial that can overwinter in cold climates, like my own.

Planting

Plant seeds four inches apart and one inch deep. Do it well after the last frost, when the soil is at least 60 degrees. For pole beans, install a trellis in your container so they can immediately start climbing. Most varieties reach maturity in sixty to seventy days. For a continuous harvest, plant seeds every two weeks throughout the summer.

Indoors. Bush beans make better indoor plants than pole beans, which need a lot of light and vertical space. Bush beans need a lot of light, too—eight to ten hours a day from a south-facing window or a grow light. But they'll never grow tall, and they self-pollinate. Water your beans only when the first inch of soil is dry. You might not get a killer harvest from indoor bush beans, but the foliage is expansive, which I like in a botanical roommate.

Upkeep

When your vining varieties reach the top of their trellis, pinch off the tips so they can focus more energy on developing and ripening pods. With their mass of luxuriant foliage, vining varieties can get thirsty, so water your beans frequently during the summer—once or even twice a day, depending on the size of your container.

For your perennials like scarlet runner beans, cut back the vine in the fall and insulate the roots with some mulch, then store your pot in a sheltered area like a garage. It's best not to water your pots through the winter to avoid stimulating the tuberous roots. But once you see spring growth, give them a long drink before moving them outside. If you don't want to keep perennial beans over the winter, dig up some of their roots, store them in a cool, dry place, and plant them again in the spring.

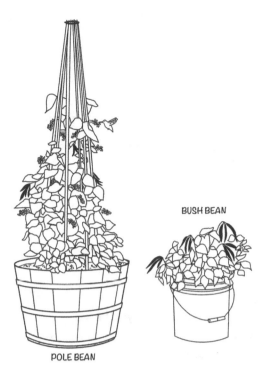

BUSH BEAN

POLE BEAN

Container gardeners tend to use dwarf varieties and bush beans interchangeably, since both are compact and don't need extra support. Pole beans, by contrast, prefer roomy planters equipped with a trellis.

Challenges

Pests. The leaves are more vulnerable to pest damage than the bean pods, which makes pest management a breeze. Even if your leaves are pocked with bug damage, the pods will remain edible and tasty. Your biggest problems will be with leafhoppers, aphids, and the copper-colored bean beetle, but no big deal—just spray the leaves with insecticidal soap.

Disease. Bacterial blights and fungal diseases can develop when conditions are too wet. Signs of disease include dark lesions on leaves, soft pods, and rotting stems. To prevent these issues, space out your plants to improve airflow and don't wet the foliage when watering. If your plant is infected, remove any diseased parts or discard the plant entirely, and change out the soil.

VEGETABLES

Harvest

Pick your beans when they're ready and you'll keep a fresh crop of beans coming in. Harvest your last crop of outdoor annuals before the first fall frost. You can enjoy tender, young beans—pod and all—or let them dry out on the vine. Dried beans can be shucked from the pod and stored in a dry cool place to add to soups, stews, and chili.

Beets

Annual
Crop type: cool

Beets are easy to grow in pots if you've got room for them. This is one vegetable I can't get enough of, so I've grown deep red Red Ace, Touchstone Gold, and the candy cane-striped Di Chioggia. Beets are biennials, which means they take two years to complete their life cycle, but treat them as annuals if you want to eat them. You only need to grow beets for a second season if you're looking to save seeds. This means that if you live in a warmer part of the country like the Southeast or West Coast and have a cold frame or greenhouse, you can continue to harvest beets throughout the winter. Otherwise, bring your pots indoors once temperatures plunge, and harvest them from your living room.

Planting

Start your seeds in early spring several weeks before the first frost date, and again in late summer for a fall or winter harvest. Beets are best sown one-half inch deep and three inches apart, in deep containers filled with well-draining soil. Mix in plenty of compost or worm castings at the time of planting and make sure no large clumps or pebbles are in the mix, since they can produce wonky-shaped roots. Thin seedlings when they're three to four inches tall, and save them for a nutritious salad topper. Crowded beets tend to be undersized.

Indoor tips. Beets are a sun-loving vegetable so unless you have large south-facing windows, sticking them under a few high-output LED grow lights is probably your best bet. Give them at least eight hours of light a day.

Upkeep

Beets need regular applications of fertilizer, but stay away from nitrogen-heavy products. Too much will encourage leafy growth over root development. (Although beet leaves *are* pretty tasty.) Once a month, feed your beets with an organic liquid fertilizer like seaweed extract, which includes boron, a mineral that beets need and potting mixes tend to leave out. This isn't necessary if you cultivate a living potting mix boosted with kelp meal. To prevent fibrous and dry roots, maintain a regular watering schedule.

Challenges

Pests. Leaf miners, aphids, and flea beetles might gnaw on your greens. Handpick them off or blast them away with a hose. A neem oil spray will also do the trick. Harvesting beet greens can prevent pest and disease problems for your plants as well, by improving air circulation.

Disease. Leaf spot, a common fungal disease that infects beets, shows up as dark blemishes on the leaves. The chances of infection are much lower for container-grown plants, but the fungus can crop up if the soil remains soggy. Allow your soil to dry out between waterings and keep the leaves dry. Thinning can help by improving airflow.

Harvest

Most beets are ready to be picked after fifty to sixty days of growing. By then, they should be about the size of a golf ball. Harvest those delicious beet greens at any time during the growing season. Remove a few outer leaves at a time by cutting the stems a few inches above the soil. Toss young, tender leaves into salads and save the older, chard-like leaves for soups and stews.

Carrots

Annual
Crop type: cool

It took me a while to find enough deep pots to grow a decent crop of carrots. Then I learned about the many blunt-shaped and baby varieties. Chunky Oxheart carrots grow only five inches long but can weigh up to one pound at maturity. Nantes carrots, a French heirloom, grow six or seven inches long and are more cylindrical. Chantenay carrots, fat and short like Oxhearts, have a deep red center. Carrots are cool-season crops best started in early spring. If you live in a climate with hot summers, wait until the end of August, when the nights have cooled, to sow another crop for fall.

Planting

Carrot seedlings are easily stressed out when transferred from one pot to another. Instead, sow seeds into containers big enough to allow them to grow, and cover the tiny seeds lightly with soil. Thin seedlings to one or two inches apart. Carrots get along well with most

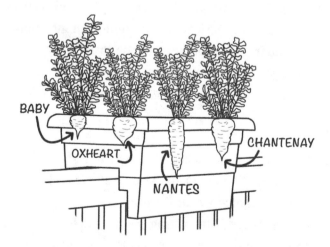

Try planting a row or two of carrots in a long railing planter, which is plenty deep enough to accommodate petite varieties such as baby, Oxheart, Nantes, and Chantenay.

VEGETABLES

plants, but keep them away from their close relative dill, because they can easily cross-pollinate and produce a bad-tasting hybrid. Dill also attracts the carrot's nemesis—the carrot rust fly.

Indoor tips. Carrots, especially mini or baby varieties, make a wonderful indoor crop. Give them plenty of light, say six to eight hours of window light or up to twelve hours under a grow light, and you can harvest them all year long.

Upkeep

Carrots prefer moist soil at all times and may need frequent drenchings during hot summer spells, especially during the early stages of growth. During periods of intense heat, place them in an area that receives some afternoon shade, since high temperatures can cause carrots to bolt. When carrots are near maturity, back off on the watering a bit to prevent growth cracks.

Challenges

Pests. Aphids, leafhoppers, and flea beetles may attack your foliage but won't do much damage below the soil. More troublesome bugs include the larvae of carrot rust flies, wireworms, carrot weevils, and click beetles that tunnel holes through roots and create black spots on your carrots. By the time you discover the damage, it's likely already too late. The best defense is prevention: Use quality soil and cover your crops with a light insect netting.

Disease. Fungal and bacterial diseases can show up as leaves that curl, or have yellow-brown or black spots. Infections spread when soil is waterlogged and the foliage stays wet. It's hard to save carrots once this happens.

Harvest

Harvest carrots at any time once they reach the size you want. Thanks to your fluffy potting soil, they'll pop out easily.

Greens (Chard, Kale, Lettuce, Spinach)

Annual and perennial
Crop type: cool
Hardiness zone: 6

Greens actually come in many shades, as reflected in a few of the varietal names, including rainbow Swiss chard and Red Rosie lettuce. Their upright, compact nature makes these plants perfect for container growing. Kale, chard, lettuce, and spinach are all cool-season veggies, so plant them outside in early spring or late summer. Some varieties of kale are perennial, living up to a few years, and can overwinter indoors or under cover outdoors, depending on the climate.

Planting

In the spring, plant your seeds into pots big enough to allow them to grow to their full size. Thin the seedlings according to package instructions. If you don't have the space outside, and want to get a head start on the season, start them in two-to-four-inch deep containers and transplant the seedlings outdoors once it's warm.

Indoors. Caring for these greens indoors is very similar to outdoor care, with the bonus of fewer pest and disease issues. But unless you have a lot of room, you probably want dwarf varieties like Dwarf Green, Curled kale, or Barese Swiss chard that reach only twelve to eighteen inches tall. Placing these greens in a south-facing window is ideal, but they'll get by on four to six hours of light from an east- or west-facing window, too. A solid Plan B is to put them under some LED grow lights.

Upkeep

Leaves get bitter in nutrient-poor or dry soils, so water your plant babies on a regular schedule and pot them in a good mix. During the growing season, I occasionally feed my plants a dose of balanced liquid fertilizer made from kelp or fish emulsion, but you don't have to if your soil contains plenty of compost. During the height of summer, move your plants where they'll get cool afternoon shade. Otherwise they might get heat stressed, bolt, and lose their fresh flavor.

Challenges

Pests. Common pests include aphids, thrips, and slugs. Check the underside of leaves regularly for clusters of these pests, and blast them off with water or spray them with neem oil. You can also sprinkle diatomaceous earth (DE) on top of the soil to prevent slugs from creeping onto plants. Draping fine netting over plants can help keep off caterpillars and other leaf-eating insects.

Disease. Diseases that can infect your greens include fungal pathogens like alternaria leaf spot and anthracnose, mold diseases like downy mildew, and bacterial diseases like black rot. Keep an eye out for dark spots or lesions of any kind and remove the infected foliage to prevent spreading. Water only when the top inch or two of soil is dry to prevent soggy conditions.

Harvest

Clip as much as you need, but leave at least a third of the plant so it has enough energy to keep growing. Avoid clipping the center, which is where your plants produce new greens. I've been able to harvest from the same lettuce patch for months without having to replant. In areas where it's mild year-round, greens can grow outdoors through the winter, and even manage occasional cold spells. I've harvested kale through a layer of snow.

Peas

Annual
Crop type: cool

Peas are an early spring crop and in-ground plants have to battle it out with cold, wet conditions every year. This means peas grown in containers have an easier go of it. The most common type is the English garden pea, which is sweet, large, and encased in pods too fibrous to eat. Snow peas are much smaller and grow inside flat edible pods. Snap peas are a cross between the two. Try growing dwarf varieties like Little Marvel English pea, Dwarf White Sugar snow pea, and Sugar Ann snap pea. Because peas are quick to mature and can fertilize soil through their nitrogen-fixing roots, they make an excellent first crop. If you successively plant these annuals, you'll be harvesting peas all year long.

Planting

If you plan to grow your peas outside, plant them in early spring or late summer when it's cool. Plant seeds one inch deep and three inches apart. In the full heat of summer, give your cool weather peas partial shade, if you can.

Indoors. Peas can grow to be three to six feet tall, which means they need to be trellised or draped over hanging pots. Even dwarf varieties need some support. Full sunlight is critical to pea growth, so if you can't provide your plants with eight hours of direct sunlight from a window, use grow lights.

Upkeep

Peas are relatively low-maintenance. All they really need is water, when the first inch or two of soil is dry. Fertilizer isn't necessary, but you can top-dress containers with some compost twice during the growing season if you'd like. To encourage the development of peas rather than leaves, stay away from nitrogen-heavy fertilizers.

Challenges

Pests. A variety of pests may attack your peas, including aphids, pea weevils, leaf miners, thrips, spider mites, and cutworms. If you notice an infestation, hose them off or spray them with insecticidal soap.

Disease. Pea plants may suffer from fungal issues like root rot, damping off, and downy mildew, which you can help prevent by keeping the foliage dry and not watering too much.

Harvest

The more pods you pick, the more your plant will produce. Pick garden peas when they've swelled enough to fill out the pod. Pick snow and snap peas when they're a few inches long and contain immature seeds. Use scissors to snip off the pods so you don't break the delicate stems.

Peppers

Tender perennial, commonly grown as an annual
Crop type: warm
Hardiness zone: 10

Peppers thrive in hot and sunny conditions and grow as perennials only in frost-free climates. You can keep them going year-round by bringing them inside before it gets cold. This is a useful growing strategy since it can take as many as one hundred long, warm summer days for peppers to mature. The most container-friendly ones may be hot pepper plants, because of their diminutive size. Super Chili, Zavory, and Orange Thai are among my favorites. Sweet peppers also come in compact varieties, including Mohawk, Arapaho, and Italico.

Planting

Start seeds indoors in early spring, six to eight weeks before the last spring frost. Consider using a heat mat, since pepper seeds need warm soil to germinate. Turn off the heat mat after they sprout. After they've grown three or four sets of leaves, move them into larger pots. A few weeks after the last frost, when nighttime temperatures are consistently at or above 55 degrees, move your containers outside. Or just buy baby plants from your local garden center.

Indoors. I bring my plants inside every fall to eke out as many peppers as I can, before they take a break and go dormant. Peppers like warmth and about eight to ten hours of direct light a day. Once they enter their resting phase, they need less light. Place your plants next to a south-facing window and—after you've picked your last pepper—trim them heavily so that only a few main branches remain. I cut mine down to no more than a ten-inch nub. The plants will grow new branches the following spring, but you'll have to add grow lights or take them outside if you want them to fruit properly. Peppers can be grown entirely indoors, but they'll never be as productive as peppers grown outside in the summer.

Upkeep

For taller pepper varieties, place a tomato cage in the pot or construct a tent trellis from stakes. Shorter varieties won't need the support, unless your peppers are in a windy area or grow top-heavy. If so, tie your plant to a sturdy stake to prevent the stem from snapping. If you overwinter your pepper plant, give it a fresh dose of compost in the spring, at least an inch deep. Since they have shallow roots, peppers can rip out of the soil if they topple over.

Challenges

Pests. Few pests will attack your peppers, though aphids can be a problem if allowed to multiply. Spray them off with soapy water or an insecticidal soap. You can also give natural predators like ladybugs a chance to eat them. Buy ladybugs in small containers—they usually arrive as unhatched eggs—and place them around your outdoor containers.

Disease. Peppers are rarely affected by disease issues, though fungal blight can crop up. There is no cure once it takes hold, but you can prune out infected leaves to prevent it from spreading to the stems. Blossom-end rot can show up as brown lesions, but the fruit is still worth harvesting. Just cut out the brown bits before eating.

Harvest

Some varieties of pepper ripen throughout the season, while others are ready all at once. You can eat all peppers green, but you'll get more flavor and nutrition if you leave them on the plant until they're fully colored. Snip them off with scissors to protect the delicate stems.

Radishes

Annual

Crop type: cool

I consider radishes an essential crop for beginner gardeners because they sprout easily and mature quickly. If you plant them in early spring before the first frost, you'll be munching on the spicy roots in as few as thirty days. Easter Egg, Cherry Belle, Pink Beauty, and Watermelon (green on the outside and bright pink on the inside) are popular spring varieties. Winter varieties are often milder in flavor, take longer to mature (forty-five to seventy days), and have a longer shelf life. Because they grow larger and longer than spring radishes, they need deeper containers. Consider winter varieties like the cylindrical and creamy white daikon radish, black Spanish radish, and Green Meat.

Planting

Though there are heat-tolerant varieties, radishes prefer the chill. The best time to sow them is a few weeks before your last spring frost date or in early fall, as soon as the nights cool. If you live in a milder, frost-free zone, you can grow them in outdoor containers all winter long. This crop likes a fluffy potting mix rich in organic matter, so don't skimp on the compost. Radishes don't do well when transplanted, so seed them directly into your container or raised bed. Poke tiny holes into your potting soil about one-quarter inch deep, and place two to three seeds into each hole. Once they've germinated, thin your seedlings to three inches apart (and eat the ones you've snipped).

Indoors. Their petite size and quick harvest time make radishes a really nice indoor crop. Sow seeds as you would outdoors and keep them well watered. Radishes like full sun, so place them next to a window that lets in direct sunlight for at least six hours a day, or directly under grow lights.

Upkeep

Because these are root crops, watering is critical. Don't let them dry out too much or they'll become tough and woody. A couple of good soaks a week will give you deeper growth. You can sow seeds every one to two weeks for a continual harvest during the cooler months.

Challenges

Pests. Many radish pests, like aphids, flea beetles, and leaf miners, attack the foliage and not the roots. But if you want to protect neighboring plants, spray these pests with an organic insecticidal soap. Slugs and maggots are more problematic since they bore holes in the roots. Maggots can also spread bacterial black spot disease. Deter slugs with a helping of diatomaceous earth (DE) and treat the maggots with Bacillus Thuringiensis (Bt) or insecticidal soap. To prevent major pest damage, cover your plants with a light row cover.

Disease. Radishes can succumb to a variety of fungal diseases, which you can generally prevent by spacing them to improve airflow and by watering the soil, not the leaves.

Harvest

Most types are ready to harvest when their root heads are about one inch wide and poke out of the soil. Pull them before they bolt. After harvesting, remove the leaves and store the roots in a vegetable crisper drawer. They can last up to two weeks.

Tomatoes

Tender perennial, commonly grown as an annual
Hardiness zone: 10
Crop type: warm

Tomatoes are pretty sensitive, which is why they make gratifying container plants. High heat can cause blossoms to fall off and frost can turn them to mush, so it's nice if you can give them an indoor, climate-controlled experience. Tomatoes grow either as vines or bushes. I prefer bush-type cherry tomatoes for container gardening because they're easy to manage. Tomatoes like long, hot summers with lots of sun, but some varieties have adapted to grow just about anywhere. In cooler climates, consider growing early-maturing varieties like Amish Gold, especially if you're growing outdoors.

Cherry tomatoes can usually be left to grow as a bushy mess. But if plants get a little top-heavy, go ahead and use sturdy bamboo stakes to keep them upright.

Planting

Since most tomatoes are heat-loving and grow slowly, I sow seeds in the early spring and move them outside when it warms up. Another option is to plant starts outside in the early summer. Much like peppers, tomatoes are true perennials only in frost-free climates. Once they're established, tomatoes are relatively drought resistant—unless they're in outdoor pots and can't reach deep into the soil for water. So water them, but not too much. Tomatoes grown without much water tend to be higher in nutritional value and more resistant to root rot and blight. Plus, they taste better because they're not as watery.

Indoors: To extend the summer growing season, bring tomatoes inside in the fall, and continue to harvest them for another couple of months or so, or until the last fruit ripens. Pots placed indoors stay moist longer, so be extra careful to let the soil dry out between waterings.

Upkeep

For vining types, prune plants back to one or two central stalks and tie each to a sturdy, six-foot bamboo stake with tomato clips or strips of an old shirt or towel. They can grow tall and floppy without proper support. As the plants grow, they'll push out suckers or new branches where the leaf meets the stem. Remove any suckers so more energy flows into the fruit-bearing central stem. If you don't get to this, no worries. You'll still have plenty of tomatoes to enjoy.

Challenges

Pests. Giant green caterpillars called tomato hornworms can quickly devour tomato leaves. You can try picking them off, but their green color makes them hard to spot, plus they're pretty juicy and gross. Use an insecticidal soap or Bt to get rid of them. They're also snacking favorites of parasitic wasps, which you can encourage by growing flowers nearby, like yarrow and asters.

The wireworm is another troublesome pest. This larval stage of the click beetle is a silent killer of newly transplanted tomatoes. If your tomatoes live in a raised bed or another large container, I recommend burying a potato attached to a stick four or five inches deep in your soil so the wire worms will go after it instead. After three weeks, dig up your potato trap and remove the worms you've captured.

Disease. Verticillium and fusarium wilts are soil-borne diseases that can kill plants fast. Once the soil has become infected, it's nearly impossible to prevent damage. If you spot signs of wilt, clear out your potting mix and start fresh next season.

Blight is a fungal disease that damages young and mature plants early or late in the season. There's little you can do about blight once plants have it, but you can keep the disease from invading the stems by removing infected leaves. Don't compost the infected leaves or the fungal infection will spread.

Harvest

Vining-type tomatoes mature in clusters throughout the growing season. Bush types tend to ripen all at once. Tomatoes are ready to harvest when they easily pop off the plant from just above the stem.

UPKEEP

I experience February a little differently from my fellow New Englanders. While I certainly put up with my share of snow, sleet, and ice storms, inside my home it feels like another world, lush and almost tropical, thanks to the thriving containers of food spread throughout.

In my kitchen, which isn't particularly well lit, I sit my aromatic herbs on the single south-facing windowsill to maximize their light. My living room, with its big sliding glass door, is where I grow fresh salad greens, root crops, and the giant kale I raised all summer and brought indoors for the winter. My bedroom holds my year-old avocado tree. And my dining room, which is relatively warm, contains my beloved fig tree and tropical lime and banana trees as well as vine-ripened cherry tomatoes, all basking in the glow of grow lights.

Watering can: I have a thing for unusual containers, which poses occasional challenges—though in this instance the adjustment was pretty minor. To provide drainage, I lined the bottom of this watering can with an inch of gravel, and slipped in a plastic pot. Done.

It's taken a few years to expand my indoor farm to this point, partly because I was nervous about taking on more work when I already felt so stretched. I used to fertilize my plants monthly and water them nonstop—at least it felt that way. But switching to a compost-rich potting mix made my job easier. I still have to remove the odd bug, but I've cut back on watering and only occasionally use fertilizer.

Over the past few years, I've developed a seasonal round of maintenance tasks that includes watering, regular pest checks, and a little weeding, in addition to feeding those hard-working soil organisms. I keep it pretty simple, and my more relaxed approach means I'll probably continue to get the occasional cracked carrot or misshapen squash, but I'm okay with that.

Consider this list a starting point. It's likely you'll want to modify it to suit your own life and your own garden, however big you want to grow it.

SPRING

This is the season to jump-start your container mini-farm by planting new annuals and potting up or replenishing some of your favorite perennials. The job can involve clearing out old pots, pruning dead and excess growth from perennials, and mixing in compost.

Prep for new plants. Experts recommend starting fresh by clearing out pots, cleaning them, and filling them with fresh potting mix. It's a way to make absolutely sure no disease carries over from the previous season. But if there were no signs of disease, it's okay to simply replenish existing potting soil by blending together equal parts new compost, or compost-heavy potting mix. If you'd like a more potent mix, add in a few soil boosters. (See "Soil boosts," page 14.)

Feed perennials. Dress your established perennials with compost or compost-rich soil mix. Add at least two inches, or as much as your containers can hold. Unless you repot your plant, it may be hard to make room for more compost given how big perennial roots can grow. Once that starts happening, I rely on EM-1, a liquid microbial inoculant, and sprinkle in granular soil amendments, like crab meal (see page 16).

Refresh raised beds. Raised beds need two things each spring: fresh compost and aeration. Before adding compost, clear any weeds. Then take a pitchfork and stab the soil every foot or so to open up pockets of air. If you need to remove soil to make room for a fresh heaping of compost, go ahead.

Mulch. Unless I'm planting directly from seed, I top my plants with a layer of organic mulch at least an inch thick, with slightly more for larger pots and raised beds. Indoor mulch won't need replenishing unless it's organic. (See "Do I mulch my newly potted plants?" page 81.)

Plant your cool-season crops. This is the time to plant radishes, lettuce, and spinach. As spring moves into summer, you can continue to grow the same crops over and over again, but move them into the shade. Or just replace them with warm-season crops. (See "Extend your harvest," page 42.)

Prune perennial plants. Cut out any dead, diseased, or broken branches from plants that have lived through the winter. Since pruning stimulates plant growth, spring is the best time to do it. Pruning is also a way to keep your plants from growing too large. I give my herbs a hard prune each spring so they don't outgrow their containers.

Keep potting soil damp, not wet. Water the soil, not the leaves or blossoms. Wet leaves invite diseases like mold and mildew, and watering the flowers can make them fall off before they can develop into fruit. Plants prefer soil that's evenly damp. (See "How often do I need to water my plants?" page 79.)

SUMMER

Summer is the time to enjoy your garden's bounty and step up your crop production, if that's your goal. You can harvest successive crops indoors, but plants simply grow more quickly when they're able to soak up direct sunlight. If you decide to move your plants outdoors to take advantage of all the light, rain, and access to microbial life and pollinators, do it gradually.

Move your plants outside. To relieve the stress of changing locations, introduce an indoor plant to the outdoors after the last spring frost. To start, allow it to sit in the sun during the day and bring it back inside at night. Do this for about a week, and your plant should settle in nicely.

Add new plants. Now's the time to replace your cool-season crops with warm-season ones, if you'd like to change things up. (See "Maximize your plot," page 39.)

Weed, if you have to. Yank weeds before they flower, because they are seed-producing machines and can quickly take over. That said, unless you're growing in a raised bed, weeds generally aren't a problem.

Water, water, water. Plants left indoors may demand more with each watering as they flower, produce fruit, and grow larger. Outdoor plants need more frequent watering to cope with the heat. If you're ever on the fence about when it's time to water, know that it's better to let a plant get a little too dry than a little too wet. (See "Is there an easy way to keep up with watering demands," page 79.)

Pollinate your indoor plants. For plants that must be pollinated to bear fruit, and don't get to frolic outdoors with insects and hummingbirds, you'll need to do it yourself once they flower. (See "How do you pollinate an indoor garden?" page 43.)

Scout for pests. No matter how small your outdoor garden, bugs will find it. They have evolved to seek out plants no matter where you've stashed them, especially if they're stressed. To keep them from doing much damage, I turn to organic solutions, like insecticidal soap or neem oil, or add barriers, like netting or row covers. (See "Indoor and outdoor organic pest solutions," page 138.)

Take steps to curb disease. Mold, mildew, and blight can wreak havoc during the summer, especially in areas with high humidity, like my hot and muggy summers in Maine. The best advice I can offer is to use potting mix that drains well, avoid overwatering, and give your plants room to breathe, which can be hard if your goal is to produce as much food as possible.

Build compost, if you can. All summer long, I stockpile untreated grass clippings, garden debris, and leaves and add them to my compost pile. I use so much, it's helpful to have a ready supply. If you don't have the outdoor space, consider building compost indoors with the help of worm roommates, or a self-composter. (See "How do I make my own compost indoors?" page 16.)

Fertilize your plants, as needed. Plants grown in compost-rich potting mix tend to do just fine without extra fertilizer. But if you want maximum efficiency from your hard-working crops, feed them additional nutrients, such as crab meal, kelp meal, or neem seed meal, or inoculate them with a microbial solution like EM-1, to help them pump out more fruit.

FALL

Fall is the season of reckoning. Which plants do you want to bring indoors? What do you leave outside? Perennials that thrive in your hardiness zone can happily stay outdoors year-round if you take steps

INDOOR AND OUTDOOR ORGANIC PEST SOLUTIONS

The goal of any organic strategy is to manage, not destroy. Full destruction usually requires the use of harsh synthetic pesticides, which kill beneficial bugs, like the bees that pollinate your raspberries or the small insects that aerate your soil, and can linger for years. Besides, even troublesome bugs have a role to play in garden ecology.

Name	What it looks like	Where it thrives
Animals	Any animal with big teeth! Birds, chipmunks, deer, rabbits, racoons, squirrels.	Outdoors
Aphids	Soft-bodied, pear-shaped bugs that are visible to the naked eye and come in a range of colors. Their sugary poop can lead to the growth of black sooty mold on your plants.	Indoors/Outdoors
Caterpillars	Larval stages of moths and butterflies can quickly grow two to three times their size and decimate foliage. Look out for pin-sized holes in leaves before they turn into large ones.	Outdoors
Flea beetles	There are many species of flea beetles. Some feed on roots, while others chew tiny holes into foliage. They are usually small, black, oval-shaped, and jump when disturbed (like fleas).	Outdoors
Fungus gnats	Tiny flies crawling on the top of soil and hovering around your plants.	Indoors
Leafhoppers	Lime-green suckers that move sideways. As they feed on plant juices, leaves exhibit light-colored speckling. Eventually, leaves curl up and turn grey or black.	Outdoors
Mealybugs	These soft-bodied bugs suck out plant sap, causing leaves to yellow and wither. They appear as tiny white, fluffy spots or in a big cottony cluster.	Indoors/Outdoors
Scale	This bug secretes a protective coating around itself (hence the name), while sucking out plant sap. Look for pinkish-orange to dark brown oval-shaped bumps that look like nasty scabs.	Indoors/Outdoors

How to spot it	What to do
Chomping on your greens, picking berry bushes clean, and digging holes in your pots.	Install a fence, hang fake predators like owls or falcons, use motion-sensored lights and sprinklers, or spray plants with smell- or taste-based repellents. Prepare yourself before spraying: The active ingredients in some organic options are rotten eggs, fish, and garlic. Good thing you don't have to use them indoors.
On the underside of leaves and on plant stems, especially around new growth.	Blast them away with water or spray them with an insecticidal soap. Signs you're getting help from parasitic wasps are aphids that look bloated or leave behind white skeletons. Gross, but good! Let their predators do the work for you.
On the underside of leaves, on plant stems, and curled up in leaf edges.	Spray Bacillus thuringiensis (Bt), use row covers, or pick them off by hand.
Pay close attention to your brassicas. Shake your plants to see if black beetles jump away. Look for a shot-hole feeding pattern, which happens when beetles chew through unfurled leaves.	Cover your plants with a floating row cover or lightweight fabric. Lure them away from vulnerable crops by planting trap crops like radish and arugula.
They love laying eggs on moist soil and feasting on decaying material. If your potting mix has compost, they're an inevitable pest. Adults don't cause any damage, but larvae can feed on plant roots and spread disease.	Allow soil to go drier in between waterings so their life cycle is cut off at the egg-laying stage. Catch adults on yellow sticky traps or bait them with an apple cider vinegar and dish soap trap.
Inspect the underside of leaves and gently shake plants to see if they jump away.	Cover your plants with row covers, spray insecticidal soap, or sprinkle on diatomaceous earth.
Common on indoor plants along stems or branches, or outdoors under fallen plant debris.	Wipe them away with a cotton ball dipped in rubbing alcohol. Spray more severe infestations with insecticidal soap.
Loves warm, dry environments. Infects not only leaves, but twigs, branches, and fruit.	Cut out severely infested stems. Insecticidal soap only works on soft-bodied insects, so spray scale with a horticultural oil. Or wipe them away with cotton balls dipped in rubbing alcohol.

Name	What it looks like	Where it thrives
Spider mites	These tiny arachnids are barely visible to the eye, but you might see webbing on your plant if there's a severe infestation. Look for stunted, curled growth, and yellow or brown stippling on leaves.	Indoors/Outdoors
Thrips	Thrips are another microscopic sap-sucker. Their damage looks like small, silvery streaks on leaves. They are oblong-shaped, slender as a sewing needle, and yellow, brown, or black in color.	Indoors/Outdoors
Whiteflies	They look like tiny gnats with powdery white wings. They feed by piercing and sucking leaves, which creates a stippling pattern. Eventually, leaves yellow and die. Whiteflies also leave behind a sticky substance called honeydew that can lead to the growth of black sooty mold.	Indoors/Outdoors

KEY TO ORGANIC PEST SOLUTIONS

DIATOMACEOUS EARTH (DE): Made from the fossils of microscopic marine life, this dusty white powder acts like killer glass shards to tiny pests. DE is effective against flea beetles, thrips, aphids, mites, and more. It will slice and dice any insect with an exoskeleton. DE is useless against cabbage worms because of their protective mucus coating. Create a ringed barrier at the base of tender seedlings or sprinkle it directly onto leaves. This product only works when leaves are dry. Make sure to buy food-grade diatomaceous earth.

BACILLUS THURINGIENSIS (BT): Bt is the name of a naturally-occurring soil-dwelling bacteria that is only toxic to butterfly and moth larvae. When caterpillars come in contact with Bt, they stop eating and starve themselves to death. Bt will kill cabbage loopers as well as monarch caterpillars, so don't let your spray drift onto non-target plants. Purchase Bt either as a concentrate or pre-mixed solution.

to protect them. With your outdoor annuals, you'll need to decide whether to harvest them now and start fresh in the spring, or bring them inside and let them ripen. I keep a few large annual pots on wheels so they're easy to cart indoors. (See "When you raise plants in pots, does your local climate matter?" page 30.)

Decide which plants to bring inside. If you live where the winters can be harsh, bring in any annuals you'd like to keep farming. Certain perennials, like raspberries and blackberries, need the cold to trigger a resting phase so it's better if they remain outside. Bring inside

How to spot it	What to do
Spider mites are often found indoors in hot and dry conditions. Look for them on the underside of leaves with a magnifying glass.	If you have a bad infestation, spray your plant with a horticultural oil or insecticidal soap.
On the underside of leaves and concentrated around tender new growth.	Spray them with horticultural oil or insecticidal soap.
Shake your plant to see if any fly away. Look for them around new growth and clustered on the underside of leaves.	Catch them with yellow sticky traps or spray with horticultural oil.

INSECTICIDAL SOAP: Use insecticidal soaps to control soft-bodied insects like aphids, mites, thrips, and mealybugs. Soap sprays break down their protective cuticles and cause fatal dehydration. The soap must come in direct contact with the pest so spray every nook and cranny of your plant. Do this on a weekly basis as new eggs hatch to prevent outbreaks. You can make your own spray by combining one tablespoon of dish soap with one quart of water.

HORTICULTURAL OIL: Either petroleum or plant-based, horticultural oils are another safe pesticide used to control soft-bodied insects as well as armored scale. My go-to product is neem oil, made from the bark and leaves of the tropical neem tree. Horticultural oils work by smothering insects to death, which means they must come in direct contact with the pest for effective control. Spray your plants on a regular basis to prevent new outbreaks. Protect beneficial bugs from harm by covering your plants while they dry.

tender perennials, like tropical fruits, or those you're growing outside of your hardiness zone, such as tomatoes and peppers, if you'd like to keep them alive through the winter.

Keep your perennials (and pots) safe outdoors. During their dormancy period, perennials hunker down and draw energy from their roots. To protect them, I blend in a couple of inches of compost and then mulch the potting soil heavily with straw. I also wrap my terra cotta and other porous containers with a thick blanket or piece of burlap to prevent them from cracking.

Plant for a year-round harvest. In temperate climates, you can grow cool-season annuals in outdoor containers all winter long. Crops you can plant outdoors for a winter harvest include chard, cabbage, beets, carrots, lettuce, and arugula. Plant them in late August or early September, to give them enough time to grow big enough to handle the colder weather.

Adjust your watering routine. Water doesn't evaporate as quickly in cool weather, and I always welcome the break the fall brings. Even if you bring plants indoors, they'll demand less water once they're out of the direct sun and wind. If they're not getting much rain or are sheltered, I keep my outdoor perennials hydrated with weekly waterings until they enter their resting phase. Indoor perennials, like my tropical fruit trees, will continue to need regular drinks—though fewer—since they keep on growing

WINTER

This is the time for many of your perennials—and maybe you?—to rest up. But if you'd rather not take a break, grow some annuals indoors. Or, if you live in a frost-free location, grow them outdoors, if they're cool-season annuals.

Look for pests. Pests are less of a problem indoors, but they can still find your plants. The most common one is the spider mite, which loves the hot, dry heat that blows up from wood stoves and floor vents. My carrots regularly hosted these uninvited mites until I finally moved them away from my baseboard heater. Other indoor bugs to watch out for are aphids, scale, white fly, thrips, and fungus gnats. (See "Indoor and outdoor organic pest solutions," page 138.)

Bring on more light. All plants, including those blessed with southern light, can benefit from grow lights as the days shorten. Set up a few grow lights above your plants, turn them on in the morning and off before going to bed, and your plants will grow more quickly and fruit more consistently. (See "What should I look for in a grow light?" page 31.)

Cut back on watering. Most outdoor perennials enter a state of dormancy during the winter. They'll likely get enough water from rain or snow, unless they're sheltering in a shed or garage. For sheltered perennials, or ones living in a warm and dry climate, water them at least monthly. For indoor plants, water them once every two weeks or so if they're in southern light. Plants under grow lights generally benefit from weekly waterings.

Dust your plants. Indoor plants accumulate dust, just like any other surface in your home. It can create a film that hinders leaf photosynthesis, and slows plant growth. Try to dust your indoor plants with a damp cloth every other month. If your plants live entirely indoors, keep up your dusting regimen all year long. To avoid damaging delicate leaves, cradle leaves in one hand and wipe off the tops with a damp cloth.

Manage for disease. Indoor plants are still vulnerable to the usual leaf spots, molds, and fungus. Again, take care to water the soil and not the plant's foliage. I use a narrow spouted watering can to target my watering, pouring only around the base of the plants.

Seasonal task list

Spring

- ☑ Prep for new plants.
- ☑ Feed perennials.
- ☑ Compost and aerate large containers.
- ☑ Add mulch.
- ☑ Plant cool-season crops.
- ☑ Prune your perennials.
- ☑ Keep soil damp, not wet.

Summer

- ☑ Move plants outside.
- ☑ Rotate in new plants.
- ☑ Weed, if necessary.
- ☑ Water, water, water.
- ☑ Pollinate indoor plants.
- ☑ Scout for pests.
- ☑ Build compost.
- ☑ Fertilize, as needed.

Fall

- ☑ Move tender plants inside.
- ☑ Tuck compost and mulch into outdoor perennials.
- ☑ Insulate fragile pots.
- ☑ Plant more cool-season crops.
- ☑ Cut back on watering.

Winter

- ☑ Look for pests indoors.
- ☑ Set up grow lights.
- ☑ Keep up indoor watering.
- ☑ Dust your plants.

QUESTIONS

I live in a tight space. What gardening tools do I really need?

If you don't have a garage, basement, or shed, it takes some finessing to manage a container garden. I mean, who wants to store a bag of compost in one of their few closets? You don't need much for a successful garden—not even extra closet space, if you mix up or buy only small bags of potting mix. If you don't have the space for a collection of gardening tools, you can always make do with a spoon for a trowel and a lemonade pitcher for a watering can. But if you can manage it, here are the tools that can make life as a container gardener a little easier.

GROW LIGHT ACCESSORIES

My favorite lights come with a clip to help secure them to a table or windowsill. For larger pots, use a tall light that hangs over your plants. You might also consider a tiered grow light stand to house all of your plants in one perfectly lit location.

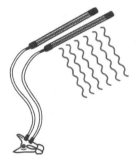

HAND PRUNER

Pruners help you clip herbs so they stay compact, or cut out dead branches on woody perennials. Good kitchen scissors can also do the job.

HARVEST BASKET

I keep my harvest in a basket, but a nice big salad bowl will hold your fresh-picked veggies just as well.

INDOOR PLANTING TRAY

Slip one of these trays under your pots to catch any debris or potting mix that spills over while you're potting up plants.

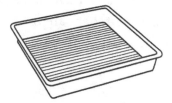

PLANT TROLLEY

Large planters are heavy and difficult to move around. Investing in a plant trolley allows you to easily move your plants from indoors to outdoors, and wheel plants aside to make room for visitors.

ROTATING FAN

The breeze can help pollinate your plants by sending pollen from one flower to another. A light wind also strengthens young seedlings so they're less likely to flop over.

SMALL TARP

A five-by-seven-foot tarp comes in handy when mixing and refreshing potting mix, and it's easy to fold and store anywhere.

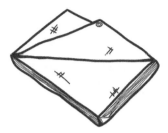

TIERED PLANT STAND

If your living room looks like mine, chances are you've run out of window room. Make the most of your prime real estate by stacking plants on a multi-level plant stand.

TROWEL

This small shovel makes it much easier to move plants in and out of containers. You can use a metal serving spoon, if you'd prefer.

WATERING CAN

I like ones with narrow spouts, which make it easier to water the soil and not the foliage. But any old pitcher will do.

ACKNOWLEDGMENTS

The other night, shortly before putting this book to bed, I invited some friends over to dinner. I watched as they scooped pink and green watermelon radishes from my salad bowl, along with miniature cucumbers and purple carrots with yellow cores—vegetables as gorgeous as they are tasty, but rarely seen in stores. I invited them to pick a couple of limes from the tree growing right next to the dinner table. And I heard them tell me that they'd love to grow their own indoor farms, if only they had the time or space, and didn't have such black thumbs.

I run into this kind of resistance all the time. One big reason I write about how I farm and garden is to reassure people that it's not that complicated. With a little planning, and that patch of light I keep referring to, it's possible for even the gardening-challenged among us to raise vegetables. The flexibility of container gardening makes it even easier.

Victory gardening is also well worth doing, even if most of us happen to live near perfectly good produce aisles and farmers' markets. By tending to our raised beds, outdoor pots, and community plots, we're making room for nature to function in a way that sustains pollinators, nourishes carbon-capturing soil organisms, and produces nutritious food. Gardeners and backyard farmers develop skills that foster self-reliance, which is comforting, especially in precarious times. Moreover, I've seen the community-building that can develop when people grow food.

Gardening is a way for each one of us to promote a healthier environment, however small our individual efforts can sometimes seem. In moments when I feel overwhelmed by the cataclysmic nature of our environmental challenges, I take inspiration from one of my heroes, the poet, essayist, and farmer Wendell Berry. He writes:

"Odd as I am sure it will appear to some, I can think of no better form of personal involvement in the cure of the environment than that of gardening. A person who is growing a garden, if he is growing it organically, is improving a piece of the world. He is producing something to eat, which makes him somewhat independent of the grocery business, but he is also enlarging, for himself, the meaning of food and the pleasure of eating."

Recently, a couple of those dinner guests who had wondered at my living room farm told me they'd pushed past their concerns, and were now growing tomatoes on their back stoop. I listened to them describe the thrill of picking their own vine-ripened tomatoes and their plans for expanding to other vegetables. It only gets better, I told them. Keep on going.

This book has been a collaboration from the start. After spending so much time working together on this, I feel like I have a new literary family.

Emily Castle simplified the act of growing in containers with her elegant graphics, charts, and illustrations. Her diligent research helped shape the plant profiles, and provided an additional level of fact-checking. I can't think of a better partner to have had by my side for this project.

Abrah Griggs brought the book to life with her expert typesetting and design. Christine McKnight lent her copy-editing expertise. And Clare Ellis—where to begin? This book wouldn't exist without her patience, faith, and vision. She took my jumbled-up ideas and gave them clarity and structure, and then tirelessly pored over the book until it was done.

And finally, to Nimbus, my loyal companion whose love helped get me through the late nights and long weekends. Yes, it's finally time to go for a nice long walk.

Good girl.

BIOS

Acadia Tucker is a regenerative farmer, climate activist, and author. Her books are a call to action to citizen gardeners everywhere, and lay the groundwork for planting an organic, regenerative garden. Acadia has published two other books with Stone Pier Press: *Growing Perennial Foods: A field guide to raising resilient herbs, fruits & vegetables*, and *Growing Good Food: A citizen's guide to climate victory gardening*.

Before becoming an author, Acadia started a four-season, organic market garden in Washington State inspired by farming pioneers Eliot Coleman and Jean-Martin Fortier. While managing the farm, Acadia grew 200 different food crops before heading back to school at the University of British Columbia to complete a Masters in Land and Water Systems. She is a Rodale Institute Ambassador for regenerative agriculture, and lives in Maine with her farm dog, Nimbus.

Emily Castle is an ecological gardener and writer based in Pennsylvania. She studied environmental science on the eastern shore of Maryland but began her love affair with plants when she visited tropical food forests abroad, becoming an instant believer in regenerative design. She currently helps propagate native plants at a botanical garden, but previously worked at an arboretum where she designed an edible and wildlife-friendly garden for children. While she takes pleasure in nurturing plants, she also enjoys illustrating them.

NOTES

NOTES

NOTES

More citizen gardening books...

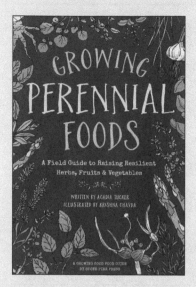

A must-have resource for home gardeners looking to take their conservation efforts to the next level. With hard-earned knowledge and conversational clarity, Tucker demystifies the concepts of regenerative agriculture, translates them to the garden level, and guides the reader both philosophically and practically.

Stephanie Anderson,
author of One Size Fits None

Great for new and experienced gardeners, *Growing Perennial Foods* is worth the purchase for the recipes alone.

Gardening Products Review

Not only does Acadia know what she's talking about, she is passionate about it.

Trish Whitinger, National Gardening Association

Beautifully written and illustrated, this book will be a well-thumbed addition to your gardening library.

The Northern Light

Acadia Tucker believes that taking cues from how plants grow in the wild will allow for cultivated gardens that produce bountiful harvests while addressing concerns about global climate change. Her guide moves through all the steps needed to create a healthy, nurturing bed.

Anne Heidemann, American Library Association

This is the best book about growing perennial vegetables I've seen.

Simply Smart Gardening

Tucker helps us tap into the deeper meaning of gardening *and* grow good food at the same time.

Anne Biklé, coauthor, The Hidden Half of Nature:
The Microbial Roots of Life and Health

My father, Wendell Berry, says that this kind of work is radical now, when public attention is focused on global solutions. This work is what people are for.

Mary Berry, Executive Director,
The Berry Center

Acadia Tucker's books are both beautiful and practical. With the approachable but extensive blueprint that she provides, you can't help but be immediately empowered and inspired to join the carbon gardening movement.

Annie Martin, Kiss the Ground

In this well-informed call to action, Acadia Tucker sets out to simplify regenerative gardening so anyone can do it. She succeeds! With step-by-step instructions and chapters dedicated to your favorite veggies, readers will be inspired to grow food and save the planet, all from the comfort of your backyard. *Jes Walton, Green America*

Tucker has a unique perspective on climate change. Working as a farmer from Washington to New Hampshire, she has seen radical shifts in climate that decimated sensitive annual crops but spared perennials. She has also seen the difference it makes to those crops when soil contains an abundance of organic material. It's a fascinating read. *Todd Heft, BBOG*

I love this book. *Growing Good Food* is great for beginner gardeners who care about the climate. *Lucy Biggers, Now This Media*

Acadia Tucker's book is an important read for any backyard grower who wants to make a positive impact on the climate in their own patch of dirt.

Robyn Rosenfeldt, Pip Magazine

Growing Good Food is a solid introduction to the larger conversation of how to make a difference on this planet with one's own land. I recommend it to every gardener.

Peggy Riccio, PegPlant

Acadia Tucker's new book shows what it takes for beginners to throw themselves into regenerative agriculture. *Lindsay Campbell, Modern Farmer*

... from Stone Pier Press

It's time to rebuild meadows wherever we
can, including the deadscape we call lawn.
Owen Wormser explains why, and how
to do this, with oodles of highly readable,
ecologically sound advice.

Douglas Tallamy, professor of entomology

I love the voicing in this book. It brought
meadows and flowers to life for me in many
ways that I am going to continue to enjoy.

*Jon Kabat-Zinn, Scientist,
writer, and founder of
Mindfulness-Based Stress Reduction*

The author tells us how to grow a meadow,
and become a positive force on behalf of the
planet. I highly recommend this book.

*Dr. John Todd, Ecologist,
author of Healing Earth*

I really like the straightforward, can-do approach of Lawns Into Meadows. This is
a really accessible, how-to book that's also about sustainability, regeneration, and
beauty. I'm so glad to get this book.

Margaret Roach, A Way to Garden, New York Times contributor

Owen Wormser shows us how to forgo grass in favor of native plant meadows, a
more climate-friendly option for your green space.   *Susannah Feltz, Bookpage*

For those interested in trading their lawn for a low-maintenance, environmentally
friendly alternative that will support wildlife and reduce pollution from mowing,
all the necessary information is here, along with plenty of sources to support it.

Anne Heidemann, Booklist

This focused and easy-to-read book is full of useful and practical information. It
contains advice on how best to prep, plant and maintain meadows, along with a
list of tools you'll need, and even guidance on how to become a meadow activist.

Permaculture Institute

Lovely book, lovely ideas, and graceful illustrations. Highly recommended.

Christopher Madden, Woodhall Press